Lecture Notes in Computer Science　　13575

More information about this series at https://link.springer.com/bookseries/558

Roxane Licandro · Andrew Melbourne ·
Esra Abaci Turk · Christopher Macgowan ·
Jana Hutter (Eds.)

Perinatal, Preterm and Paediatric Image Analysis

7th International Workshop, PIPPI 2022
Held in Conjunction with MICCAI 2022
Singapore, September 18, 2022
Proceedings

Springer

Editors
Roxane Licandro 🆔
Massachusetts General Hospital & Harvard
Medical School
Charlestown, MA, USA

Medical University of Vienna
Vienna, Austria

Esra Abaci Turk
Children's Hospital
Boston, MA, USA

Jana Hutter 🆔
King's College London
London, UK

Andrew Melbourne 🆔
King's College London
London, UK

Christopher Macgowan 🆔
The Hospital for Sick Children Research
Institute
Toronto, ON, Canada

ISSN 0302-9743   ISSN 1611-3349 (electronic)
Lecture Notes in Computer Science
ISBN 978-3-031-17116-1   ISBN 978-3-031-17117-8 (eBook)
https://doi.org/10.1007/978-3-031-17117-8

This Springer imprint is published by the registered company Springer Nature Switzerland AG
The registered company address is: Gewerbestrasse 11, 6330 Cham, Switzerland

Preface

The goal of the Perinatal, Preterm and Paediatric Image Analysis (PIPPI) workshop is to provide a focused platform for the discussion and dissemination of advanced imaging techniques applied to young cohorts. The technical program typically consists of one keynote talk from a prominent figure in the community and the presentation of previously unpublished papers. Emphasis is placed on novel methodological approaches to the study of, for instance, volumetric growth, myelination and cortical microstructure, and placental structure and function or the assessment of new technical innovations for planned intervention. Although techniques applied to MR neuroimaging provide a significant number of submissions, we are delighted to receive submissions making use of other modalities or applied to other target organs or regions of interest such as the fetal heart and the placenta.

The main objective of PIPPI is to provide a forum for researchers in the MICCAI community to discuss the challenges of image analysis techniques as applied to the preterm, perinatal and paediatric setting which are confounded by the interrelation between the normal developmental trajectory and the influence of pathology. These relationships can be quite diverse when compared to measurements taken in adult populations and exhibit highly dynamic changes affecting both image acquisition and processing requirements. Furthermore, this forum will facilitate the presentation and detailed discussion of novel and speculative works, which may be outside the scope of the main conference but are essential for the advancement of modeling and analysis of medical imaging data. Additionally, discussion of these works within a focused group may initiate new collaborations.

The application of sophisticated analysis tools to fetal, neonatal, and paediatric imaging data has gained additional interest, especially in recent years with the successful large-scale open data initiatives such as the developing Human Connectome Project, the Baby Connectome Project, and the NIH-funded Human Placenta Project. These projects enable researchers without access to perinatal scanning facilities to bring in their image analysis expertise and domain knowledge.

This year's workshop took place on September 18, 2022, as a satellite event of the 25th International Conference on Medical Image Computing and Computer Assisted Intervention (MICCAI 2022). Two keynote speakers – Ting Xu (Child Mind Institute, New York, USA) and Gentaro Taga (University of Tokyo, Japan) – were invited for PIPPI 2022 to stimulate discussions, present recent research, and highlight future challenges in this field. Speakers working at the interface of clinical relevance and technical competence ensure close connection between technical, methodological research and clinical applications.

Following our experiences from the workshops in 2020 and 2021, PIPPI 2022 made use of a hybrid setup, allowing participants to join either in person or online. The online set up of the workshops in 2020 and 2021 had several successful elements, allowing the participation of traditionally non-MICCAI attendees (clinicians, scientists) and the inclusion of a clinical keynote, and also helping to widen participation for those unable to travel. Continuing these elements improved the participation and accessibility of our workshop, whilst not adversely influencing the traditional workshop format for those attending on site. On site oral presentations were recorded live whilst virtual presentations were projected. All presented posters were displayed in joint virtual and physical settings.

As part of our changes for 2022, PIPPI has enhanced the links with researchers working in Computer Assisted Intervention (CAI). This is becoming increasingly relevant to PIPPI as fetal and neonatal interventions become more complex and new surgical developments lead to highly specialized tools and advanced methods for surgical planning.

This year, PIPPI saw the introduction of a new session format, the PIPPI Circle, a forum for open discussion among different communities researching early life. This session brought together scientists from clinics, industry, and academia to form a round-table panel to discuss the most pressing challenges in fetal and paediatric imaging, future directions for research, and the clinical requirements from the user's and patient's perspective.

PIPPI 2022 continued the support of the Fetal Tissue Annotation and segmentation (FeTA) challenge [1] and also added a new challenge, the BabySteps 2022 challenge [2]. Roxane Licandro and Jana Hutter acted as coordinators between the PIPPI workshop organizing team and the FeTA and BabySteps challenge team, respectively.

Teaming up with the ISMRM Placenta & Fetus study group, and having Christopher Macgowan as both an organizer of PIPPI and the study group committee chair, has allowed PIPPI to foster more interactions between related but often separated fields, enabling researchers with joint interests in perinatal imaging but with diverse backgrounds to meet, interact, and develop new collaborations. Concrete topics of focus include motion correction and fetal cardiac imaging, topics of huge importance for the community and where excellent expertise is present within the ISMRM community.

This year PIPPI teamed up with the FIT'NG (Fetal Infant Toddler Neuroimaging Group) network, an organization devoted to the study of brain development during the fetal, infant, and toddler periods. This enabled the workshop to have access to an additional community and supported the popular PIPPI topic of neuroimaging, by providing both reviewers and access to the widely distributed FIT'NG network.

PIPPI 2022 received original, innovative, and mathematically rigorous papers for the analysis of both imaging data and the application of surgical and interventional techniques applied to fetal and paediatric conditions. The methods presented in these papers, and hence these proceedings, cover the full scope of medical image analysis: segmentation, registration, classification, reconstruction, atlas construction, tractography, population analysis and advanced structural, and functional and longitudinal modeling, all with an application to younger cohorts or to the long-term outcomes of perinatal conditions. All papers were reviewed by three expert reviewers from the Program Committee and ten papers were selected for presentation at PIPPI 2022 and are thus included in these proceedings. We are grateful to everyone who helped make this year's workshop a success.

September 2022

Jana Hutter
Roxane Licandro
Andrew Melbourne
Esra Abaci Turk
Christopher Macgowan

References

1. Payette, K., Steger, C., de Dumast, P., Jakab, A., Cuadra, M.B., Vasung, L., Licandro, R., Barkovich, M., Li, H.: Fetal Tissue Annotation Challenge (March 16, 2022). https://doi.org/10.5281/zenodo.6683366.
2. Edwards, A.D., Rueckert, D., Smith, S.M., Abo Seada, S., Alansary, A., Almalbis, J., Allsop, J., Andersson, J., Arichi, T., Arulkumaran, S., Bastiani, M., Batalle, D., Baxter, L., Bozek, J., Braithwaite, E., Brandon, J., Carney, O., Chew, A., Christiaens, D., Chung, R., Colford, K., Cordero-Grande, L., Counsell, S.J., Cullen, H., Cupitt, J., Curtis, C., Davidson, A., Deprez, M., Dillon, L., Dimitrakopoulou, K., Dimitrova, R., Duff, E., Falconer, S., Farahibozorg, S-R., Fitzgibbon, S.P., Gao, J., Gaspar, A., Harper, N., Harrison, S.J., Hughes, E.J., Hutter, J., Jenkinson, M., Jbabdi, S., Jones, E., Karolis, V., Kyriakopoulou, V., Lenz, G., Makropoulos, A., Malik, S., Mason, L., Mortari, F., Nosarti, C., Nunes, R.G., O'Keeffe, C., O'Muircheartaigh, J., Patel, H., Passerat-Palmbach, J., Pietsch, M., Price, A.N., Robinson, E.C., Rutherford, M.A., Schuh, A., Sotiropoulos, S., Steinweg J., Teixeira R.P.A.G., Tenev T., Tournier J-D., Tusor N., Uus A., Vecchiato K., Williams L.Z.J., Wright R., Wurie J. and Hajnal J.V.: The Developing Human Connectome Project Neonatal Data Release. Frontiers in Neurocience 16 (2022). https://doi.org/10.3389/fnins.2022.886772.

Organization

Program Committee Chairs

Jana Hutter   King's College London, UK

Roxane Licandro   Medical University of Vienna, Austria, and MGH, Harvard Medical School, USA

Andrew Melbourne   King's College London, UK

Esra Abaci Turk   Boston Children's Hospital, USA

Christopher Macgowan   University of Toronto, Canada

Program Committee

Alena Uus   King's College London, UK

Athena Taymourtash   Medical University of Vienna, Austria

Daniel Sobotka   Medical University of Vienna, Austria

Dimitra Flouri   King's College London, UK

Elisenda Eixarch   Barcelona Children's Hospital, Spain

Gemma Piella   Universitat Pompeo Fabra, Spain

Hongwei Li   TU Munich, Germany, and University of Zurich, Switzerland

Jeffrey N. Stout   Boston Children's Hospital, USA

Kelly M. Payette   Children's Hospital Zurich, Switzerland, and MGH, Harvard Medical School, USA

Lana Vasung   Boston Children's Hospital, USA

Lilla Zöllei   MGH, Harvard Medical School, USA

Logan Z. J. Williams   King's College London, UK

Malte Hoffmann   MGH, Harvard Medical School, USA

Mazdak Abulnaga   MIT, USA

Pablo-Miki Martí   Universitat Pompeo Fabra, Spain

Veronika A. Zimmer   TU Munich, Germany

Contents

Automatic Segmentation of the Placenta in BOLD MRI Time Series

S. Mazdak Abulnaga[1]([✉]), Sean I. Young[1,2], Katherine Hobgood[1], Eileen Pan[1], Clinton J. Wang[1], P. Ellen Grant[3], Esra Abaci Turk[3], and Polina Golland[1]

[1] Computer Science and Artificial Intelligence Lab, Massachusetts Institute of Technology, Cambridge 02139, USA
{abulnaga,siyoung,khobgood,eileenp}@mit.edu,
{clintonw,polina}@csail.mit.edu

[2] MGH/HST Martinos Center for Biomedical Imaging, Harvard Medical School, Boston, MA 02129, USA

[3] Fetal-Neonatal Neuroimaging and Developmental Science Center, Boston Children's Hospital, Harvard Medical School, Boston, MA 02115, USA
{ellen.grant,esra.abaciturk}@childrens.harvard.edu

Abstract. Blood oxygen level dependent (BOLD) MRI with maternal hyperoxia can assess oxygen transport within the placenta and has emerged as a promising tool to study placental function. Measuring signal changes over time requires segmenting the placenta in each volume of the time series. Due to the large number of volumes in the BOLD time series, existing studies rely on registration to map all volumes to a manually segmented template. As the placenta can undergo large deformation due to fetal motion, maternal motion, and contractions, this approach often results in a large number of discarded volumes, where the registration approach fails. In this work, we propose a machine learning model based on a U-Net neural network architecture to automatically segment the placenta in BOLD MRI and apply it to segmenting each volume in a time series. We use a boundary-weighted loss function to accurately capture the placental shape. Our model is trained and tested on a cohort of 91 subjects containing healthy fetuses, fetuses with fetal growth restriction, and mothers with high BMI. We achieve a Dice score of 0.83 ± 0.04 when matching with ground truth labels and our model performs reliably in segmenting volumes in both normoxic and hyperoxic points in the BOLD time series. Our code and trained model are available at https://github.com/mabulnaga/automatic-placenta-segmentation.

Keywords: Placenta · Segmentation · BOLD MRI · CNN

1 Introduction

The placenta is an organ that provides oxygen and nutrients to support fetal growth. Placental dysfunction can cause pregnancy complications and can affect fetal development, so there is a critical need to assess placental function *in vivo*.

R. Licandro et al. (Eds.): PIPPI 2022, LNCS 13575, pp. 1–12, 2022.
https://doi.org/10.1007/978-3-031-17117-8_1

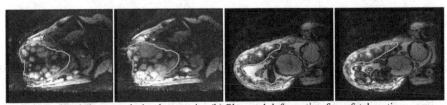

(a) BOLD signals increase during hyperoxia   (b) Placental deformation from fetal motion

Fig. 1. Example images and placental segmentations: (a) signal brightening during hyperoxia, and (b) shape deformation caused by fetal motion. Placental boundaries are marked in yellow. Areas outside of the placenta are darkened for illustration. Intensity scale is based on the first MRI volume in the time series. (Color figure online)

Blood oxygen level dependent (BOLD) MRI can directly quantify oxygen transport within the placenta [3,16] and has emerged as a promising tool to study placental function. Temporal analysis of BOLD MRI with maternal oxygenation has been used to identify contractions [1,13], biomarkers of fetal growth restriction [7,15], predict placental age [10] and to study congenital heart disease [18,24] among many uses.

Despite its importance for many downstream clinical research tasks, placental segmentation is often performed manually and can take a significant amount of time, even for a trained expert. For BOLD MRI studies, manual segmentation is rendered more challenging due to the sheer number of MRI scans acquired and rapid signal changes due to the experimental design. Experiments acquire several hundred whole-uterus MRI scans to observe signal changes in three stages: i) normoxic (baseline), ii) hyperoxic, and iii) return to normoxic. During the hyperoxic stage, the BOLD signals increase rapidly, leading to hyperintensity throughout the placenta. Furthermore, the placental shape can undergo large deformation caused by maternal breathing, contractions, and fetal motion which can be particularly increased during hyperoxia [25]. See Fig. 1 for two examples.

The current practice is to analyze BOLD signals with respect to one template volume. Deformable registration of all volumes in the time series to the template is performed to enable spatiotemporal analysis [2,25]. However, due to significant motion, registration can lead to large errors, requiring outlier detection and possibly rejecting a significant number of volumes [2,25].

To address these challenges, we propose a model to automatically segment the placenta in BOLD MRI time series. Our model is trained on several volumes from each patient during the normoxic and hyperoxic phases, to capture the nuanced placental changes. We apply our model on unseen BOLD MRI volumes to demonstrate consistency in the predicted segmentation label maps. Our method performs favorably against the state-of-the-art on a large dataset with a broad range of gestational ages and pregnancy conditions. Automatic segmentation is necessary for whole-organ signal analysis, and can be used to improve time-series registration to enable localized analysis. Furthermore, it is an essential step in several post-processing tasks, including motion correction [2], reconstruction [21], and mapping to a standardized representation [4,8].

Machine learning segmentation models for the placenta have been previously proposed and include both semi-automatic [23] and automatic [5,10,17,19] approaches. While semi-automatic methods have achieved success in predicting segmentation label maps with high accuracy, these approaches are infeasible for segmenting BOLD MRI time series due to the large number of volumes. The majority of automatic methods focus on segmentation in anatomical images. Alansary et al. [5] proposed a model for segmenting T2-weighted (T2w) images based on a 3D CNN followed by a dense CRF for segmentation refinement and validated on a singleton cohort that included patients with fetal growth restriction (FGR). Torrents-Barrena et al. [19] proposed a model based on super-resolution and an SVM and validated on a singleton and twin cohort of T2w MRI. Spektor-Fadida et al. [17] tackled the problem of domain transfer by a self-training model and demonstrated successful segmentation of FIESTA and TRUFI sequences. For a more detailed treatment of segmentation methods in fetal MRI, we refer the reader to the survey by Torrents-Barrena et al. [20].

Functional images of the placenta differ greatly from anatomical images, as they have lower in-plane resolution and the contrast between the placental boundary and surrounding anatomy is less pronounced. Anatomical images may also benefit from super-resolution approaches to increase SNR in the acquired image [21]. Pietsch et al. [10] are the first to consider placental segmentation in functional MRI. They proposed a 2D patch-based U-Net model for functional image segmentation and demonstrated a successful application of age prediction using the estimated T2* values. They focused on a cohort of singleton subjects, and demonstrated success on abnormal pregnancy conditions including preeclampsia. In contrast to their approach that segments derived T2* maps, we evaluate our segmentation model on BOLD MRI time series. Furthermore, our 3D model operates on the entire volume rather than patches, thereby helping to better resolve the boundaries of the placenta.

To capture the large signal changes and placental shape variation in the time series, we train with a random sampling of manual segmentations of several volumes in the BOLD MRI series. We propose a boundary weighted loss function to more easily identify the placental boundary and improve segmentation accuracy. Finally, to evaluate the feasibility of our method for clinical research, we propose additional metrics to evaluate performance on the whole MRI time series, and illustrate a possible clinical research application.

2 Methods

We aim to find a model $F_\theta : X \rightarrow Y$ that takes a BOLD MRI time series $X \in \mathbb{R}^{T \times H \times W \times D}$ and predicts a set of placenta segmentation label maps for each time point $t \in \{1, \ldots T\}$, $Y \in \{0,1\}^{T \times H \times W \times D}$, where T is the total number of time points at which MRI scans were acquired. For a given BOLD time series, we have a small number N_l of frames with ground truth labels $(\mathbf{x}, \mathbf{y})$, where $\mathbf{x} \in \mathbb{R}^{H \times W \times D}$ is an MRI scan and $\mathbf{y} \in \{0,1\}^{H \times W \times D}$ is the ground truth placenta label map.

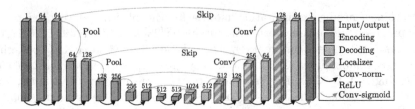

Fig. 2. 3D Placenta Segmentation U-Net. We use a five-level 3D U-Net with max-pooling, skip connections, and convolution-transpose layers. Numbers above vertical bars denote the number of features at various stages of the processing pipeline. Batch norm is employed for normalization (batch size = 8).

2.1 Model

We use a 3D U-Net [12] with 4 blocks in the contracting and expanding paths. Each block consists of two sets of $3 \times 3 \times 3$ convolution with ReLU activations, followed by max pooling (contraction path) or transpose convolution (expansion path), as illustrated in Fig. 2. We augment the images using random affine transforms, flips, whole-image brightness shifts, contrast changes, random noise, and elastic deformations, using TorchIO [11]. We simulate the effects of maternal normoxia and hyperoxia with a constant intensity shift in the placenta.

To capture the MRI signal and placental shape changes resulting from maternal hyperoxia and fetal motion, we enhance our training with several manually segmented volumes in the normoxic or hyperoxic phase. This allows the model to learn from the realistic variations that arise during maternal oxygenation.

2.2 Additive Boundary Loss

The placental boundary can be difficult to distinguish in BOLD MRI scans due to similar appearance with surrounding anatomy. To emphasize the boundary details, we construct an additive boundary-weighting W to the segmentation loss function L. Given a ground truth placental label map $\mathbf{y}$, we denote its boundary as $\partial\mathbf{y}$. We use a signed distance function $f(x)$ that measures the signed distance, $d(x, \partial\mathbf{y})$, of voxel $x \in \mathbb{R}^3$ to the boundary, where $f(x) < 0$ when outside of the placenta and $f(x) > 0$ when inside. The boundary weighting is additive for voxels within δ-distance of $\partial\mathbf{y}$,

$$W_\delta(x) = \begin{cases} w_1 & \text{if } -\delta < f(x) < 0, \\ w_2 & \text{if } \quad 0 \le f(x) < \delta, \\ 0 & \text{otherwise.} \end{cases} \tag{1}$$

The weighted-loss is then

$$L_w(x) = L(x)\left[1 + W_\delta(x)\right]. \tag{2}$$

In practice, we set $w_1 > w_2$, to penalize outside voxels more heavily and learn to distinguish the placenta from its surrounding anatomy. To find voxels with

$|f(x)| < \delta$, we estimate a 2δ-wide boundary by an average pooling filter on $\mathbf{y}$ with kernel size K and take the smoothed outputs to lie in the boundary. A larger K produces a wider boundary, penalizing more misclassified voxels.

2.3 Implementation Details

We train using a learning rate $\eta = 10^{-4}$ for 3000 epochs and select the model with the best Dice score on the validation set. For the additive boundary loss, we set $w_1 = 40$, $w_2 = 1$, and $K = 11$. All volumes are normalized by mapping the 90th percentile intensity value to 1. We use a batch size of 8 MRI volumes. We crop or pad all volumes in the dataset to have dimension $112 \times 112 \times 80$, and train on the entire 3D volume. We augment our data with random translations of up to 10 voxels, rotations up to $22°$, Gaussian noise sampled with $\mu = 0, \sigma = 0.25$, elastic deformations with 5 control points and a maximum displacement of 10 voxels, whole volume intensity shifts up to $\pm 25\%$, and whole-placenta intensity shifts of ± 0.15 normalized intensity values. These values were determined by cross-validation on the training set. When evaluating the model on our test set, we post-processed produced label maps by taking the largest connected component to eliminate islands. Our code and trained model are available at https://github.com/mabulnaga/automatic-placenta-segmentation.

3 Model Evaluation

3.1 Data

Our dataset consists of BOLD MRI scans taken from two clinical research studies. Data was collected from 91 subjects of which 78 were singleton pregnancies (gestational age (GA) at MRI scan of 23wk5d – 37wk6d), and 13 were monochorionic-diamniotic (Mo-Di) twins (GA at MRI scan of 27wk5d – 34wk5d). Of these, 63 were controls, 16 had fetal growth restriction (FGR), and 12 had high BMI (BMI > 30). Obstetrical ultrasound was used to classify subjects with FGR. For singleton subjects, classification was done based on having fetuses with estimated weight less than the 10th percentile. For twin subjects, FGR classification was determined by provene monoochorionicity and discordance in the estimated fetal weight by i) growth restriction ($<10^{\text{th}}$ percentile) in one or both fetuses; and/or ii) growth discordance ($\geq 20\%$) between fetuses. Table 1 shows patient demographics and GA ranges per group.

MRI BOLD scans were acquired on a 3T Siemens Skyra scanner (GRE-EPI, interleaved with 3 mm isotropic voxels, TR = 5.8–8 s, TE = $32 - 47$ ms, FA = $90°$). To eliminate intra-volume motion artifacts, we split the acquired interleaved volumes into two separate volumes with spacing $3 \times 3 \times 6$ mm, then linearly interpolate to $3 \times 3 \times 3$ mm. In our analysis, we only consider one of two split volumes. Maternal oxygen supply was alternated during the BOLD acquisition via a nonrebreathing facial mask to have three 10-min or 5-min consecutive episodes: 1. Normoxic ($21\% \ O_2$), 2. Hyperoxic ($100\% \ O_2$, 15 L/min), 3. Normoxic

Table 1. Subject demographic information.

Group	Control	FGR	High BMI
Singleton: N subj.	60	6	12
GA at MRI	23wk5d – 37wk6d	26wk6d – 34wk5d	26wk4d – 36wk6d
Twin: N subj.	3	10	0
GA at MRI	31wk2d – 34wk5d	27wk5d – 34wk5d	N/A

(21% O_2). The placenta was manually segmented by a trained observer. Each BOLD MRI time series had 1 to 6 manual segmentations, yielding a total of 176 ground truth labels. The data was split into a training, validation, and test sets: (65%/15%/20%: 63/11/17 subjects) and stratified on pregnancy condition.

Each subject in the training set had up to $N_l = 6$ ground truth segmentations in the BOLD time series. To prevent the model from being biased by subjects with more ground truth labels, we train by randomly sampling one of N_l ground truth segmentations in each epoch.

3.2 Evaluation

We first compare the predicted segmentation label maps to ground truth segmentations. We measure similarity using the Dice score (Dice), the 95th-percentile Hausdorff distance (HD95), and the Average Symmetric Surface Distance (ASSD). To evaluate the feasibility of the produced segmentations for clinical research studying whole-organ signal changes, we evaluate the relative error in the mean BOLD values, defined as $|\hat{b} - b|/b$, where b and $\hat{b}$ denote the mean BOLD signal in the ground truth and in the predicted segmentation, respectively.

We evaluate several variants of our model using these metrics. We assess the effect of the boundary-weighting (BW) loss term and compare performance using the Cross-entropy (CE), Dice [9], and Focal [6] loss functions. We evaluate the generalization ability by comparing with the model trained on only the first of N_l BOLD frames and without random sampling of labeled segmentations.

We evaluate our model's sensitivity to oxygenation by comparing the accuracy of predictions in the normoxic and hyperoxic phases for a given subject. We compute the absolute difference of the similarity metric m between an image in normoxia and in hyperoxia, $|m_{normoxic}(\mathbf{y}, \hat{\mathbf{y}}) - m_{hyperoxic}(\mathbf{y}, \hat{\mathbf{y}})|$, where $m_{normoxic}(\mathbf{y}, \hat{\mathbf{y}})$ denotes the similarity between our predicted segmentation $\hat{\mathbf{y}}$ and the ground truth $\mathbf{y}$ using the metric m for an image in the normoxic phase. We use the Dice score, HD95, ASSD, and relative BOLD error for m.

We assess the consistency of our predictions by applying our model to all volumes in the BOLD time series of the test set. Since our volumes are acquired interleaved and split into two separate volumes, we apply our model to every second volume in the time series, yielding a mean of 111.7 ± 45.3 volumes per subject. We measure consistency by comparing the Dice score, HD95, ASSD, and normalized BOLD difference between consecutive volumes.

Finally, we demonstrate a possible application of temporal analysis by measuring increases in mean BOLD signal during hyperoxia.

Table 2. Test results produced by our 3D U-Net model trained using different loss functions. Numbers in bold indicate the best result in each column.

Loss	Dice score	HD95 (mm)	ASSD (mm)	BOLD diff
BW-CE	**0.83 ± 0.04**	13.36 ± 6.08	**4.06 ± 0.97**	0.051 ± 0.025
BW-CE + Dice	0.82 ± 0.04	13.34 ± 5.43	4.16 ± 0.99	0.050 ± 0.043
BW-Focal	0.82 ± 0.04	13.52 ± 5.54	4.15 ± 0.98	**0.046 ± 0.033**
BW-CE ($N_l = 1$)	0.81 ± 0.05	**13.26 ± 5.98**	4.38 ± 1.35	0.057 ± 0.033
BW-Focal + Dice	0.78 ± 0.19	22.16 ± 36.25	11.67 ± 29.55	0.103 ± 0.239
CE (no BW)	0.76 ± 0.07	18.26 ± 11.64	6.04 ± 2.21	0.051 ± 0.027

3.3 Results

Table 2 reports the performance of several variants of our model on the test set. Our best model achieves a Dice score of 0.83 ± 0.04 with a HD95 = 13.36 ± 6.08 mm using the BW-CE loss. Further, we achieve low relative BOLD error (0.051±0.025), indicating that our model's segmentations are suitable for clinical research studies assessing whole-organ signal changes. Similar performance is achieved for the other loss functions. Training the model without the boundary weighting (Eq. (2)) results in a statistically significant drop in performance, achieving a Dice of 0.76 ($p < 10^{-4}$ using a paired t-test). Using only the first segmented volume of the BOLD MRI series ($N_l = 1$) in the normoxic phase also results in a significant drop in performance, achieving a Dice of 0.81 ($p < 0.05$). Adding labeled examples in the hyperoxic phase helps generalization, as the placental shape and intensity patterns can change greatly.

Our performance is consistent across pregnancy conditions, as we achieve Dice scores of (0.76, 0.89) on the two subjects with twin pregnancies, 0.83 ± 0.04 on the singletons (N = 15), 0.83 ± 0.07 on the FGR cohort (N = 3), 0.82 ± 0.04 on the controls (N = 12) and (0.84, 0.88) on the two BMI cases.

Direct comparison of this work to previous studies is not feasible due to differences in data set size and patient demographics, imaging protocols, and MRI study design. The current state-of-the-art automatic segmentation method for functional MRI (T2*) achieves a Dice score of 0.58 on a cohort of low- and high-risk singleton subjects of a wide GA range [10]. Their performance was comparable to the inter-rater variability of two radiologists (Dice = 0.68), which represents an upper limit. In their work, they trained on a combination of T2* weighting and BOLD sequences, while we focus only on BOLD.

Our model performs consistently well in the normoxic and hyperoxic phases. For the 5 subjects with ground truth segmentations in both the normoxic and hyperoxic phase, we achieve a mean absolute difference between predictions in normoxia and hyperoxia of 0.026 ± 0.02 Dice, 5.69 ± 2.33 mm HD95, 0.75 ± 0.46 mm ASSD, and 0.06±0.04 relative BOLD error. These results suggest that our model is robust to contrast changes in the placenta resulting from maternal hyperoxia, and can be used in studies quantifying oxygen transport in the organ. A larger number of subjects are needed to assess statistical significance.

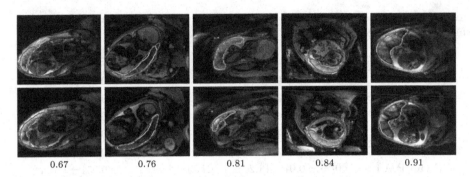

| 0.67 | 0.76 | 0.81 | 0.84 | 0.91 |

Fig. 3. Example predictions on 5 subjects from the test set. Ground truth segmentations are shown in yellow and predictions in red. Dice scores are indicated below each column. Two slices are shown for each subject, spaced 18 mm apart. (Color figure online)

Figure 3 compares the predicted label maps with ground truth on 5 subjects with increasing Dice scores using the BW-CE model. The model accurately identifies the location of the placenta, but in the worst cases misses boundary details.

BOLD Time Series Evaluation. Table 3 presents statistics of the consistency between predicted label maps in consecutive volumes of the MRI time series. Predictions are highly consistent, achieving a Dice of 0.92 ± 0.02. The small differences between the relative mean-BOLD values suggest these produced segmentations may be suitable for research studies assessing placental function.

Figure 4 presents distributions of Dice score between predicted label maps of consecutive frames in the BOLD time series. Distributions have high medians (>0.9) for all but one case, with wide density at high Dice scores (>0.9. Dice differences are highly affected by fetal and maternal motion that causes placental deformation. We visually verified that modest drops in Dice (<0.9) were mainly due to fetal motion, but large drops (Dice < 0.7) resulted from errors in the produced label maps.

Automatic segmentation of each volume in BOLD MRI time series is advantageous as it can enable whole-organ spatiotemporal analysis without requiring inter-volume motion correction or registration, which may fail under the presence of large motion. We illustrate one possible application by investigating the percentage increase in BOLD signal in response to maternal hyperoxia. We calcu-

Table 3. Consistency of predictions in the BOLD time series produced by our best-performing 3D U-Net model (trained using the BW-CE loss function).

Measure	Dice score	HD95 (mm)	ASSD (mm)	BOLD diff
Consistency across consecutive frames	0.92 ± 0.02	5.69 ± 2.33	1.94 ± 0.05	0.021 ± 0.007

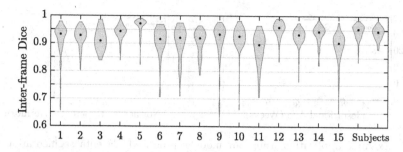

Fig. 4. Per-subject density distributions of Dice scores between consecutive predictions in BOLD MRI time series. Dots inside distributions indicate the median.

late the percentage increase over the baseline period: $\Delta b = |b_H - b_N|/b_N$, where b_N denotes the mean BOLD signal over the baseline period, and b_H denotes the mean of the signal in the last 10 frames of the hyperoxic period.

Figure 5 shows a scatter plot of the hyperoxia response for all subjects in the test set and two examples of the BOLD signal time course in the produced placenta segmentation label maps. In the control subjects (N = 12), we observe an increase of $10.2 \pm 11.1\%$. The observed increase for the healthy controls is consistent with previous studies that demonstrated an increase of $12.6 \pm 5.4\%$ (N = 21) [15] and from 5% to 20% throughout gestation (N = 49) [14].

4 Discussion and Conclusion

We developed a model to automatically segment placental scans in BOLD MRI and achieve close matching to ground truth labels with consistent performance in predicting volumes in both the normoxic and hyperoxic phases. Key to our model development is a boundary-weighted loss function and training with labeled volumes obtained at different oxygenation phases in the BOLD MRI time series.

Segmenting each volume in the BOLD MRI time series can be advantageous for clinical research assessing whole-organ changes as it eliminates the need for registration. Registration algorithms are affected by fetal motion and may require discarding a significant number of volumes [2,25], potentially losing important signal information. We illustrate one possible study in assessing placental response during hyperoxia, observing an increase in signal intensity consistent with prior work. However, our cohort is limited, and several factors, including maternal position, gestational age, and contractions are covariates not considered.

Registration however is advantageous for localized analysis [2], and solely relying on segmentation would only permit quantifying whole-organ signal changes, for example mean T2* or mean BOLD increase. Placental segmentations can be incorporated into registration methods as spatial priors to improve registration results. Future work will investigate joint segmentation-registration models.

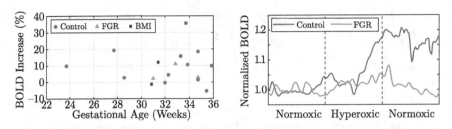

Fig. 5. Example application using our model's produced placenta segmentations in BOLD time series to characterize oxygenation response from maternal hyperoxia. Left: observed increase relative to baseline for the test set. Right: example time series for one singleton control (GA = 33wk2d, Dice = 0.84, Δb = 15.7%) and one singleton FGR subject (GA = 34wk5d, Dice = 0.84, Δb = 2.9%).

We assessed the consistency of predictions in BOLD MRI time series using our model, and achieved highly consistent predictions (Dice = 0.92). For many subjects, we observed modest drops in Dice (<0.9), which were often due to fetal motion displacing the placenta. However, in a small number of cases, we observed large drops (Dice < 0.7) that we visually verified were caused by segmentation error. Since we apply the model to each volume in the time series independently, imaging artifacts, such as intensity and geometric artifacts, can affect the predicted segmentations. In future work, we will investigate incorporating temporal consistency between consecutive volumes. We will also investigate applying test-time augmentation on image intensity as this has been shown to reduce uncertainty and improve segmentation robustness [22].

Key to our model performance was maximizing data variability by having manually segmented volumes at different points in the BOLD MRI series. Future work will investigate semi-supervised learning to incorporate all unlabeled volumes. As there are often in the order of 100 unlabeled volumes in each BOLD time series, these approaches can more accurately capture the rapid signal changes resulting from fetal motion and maternal oxygenation.

Future directions of this work will investigate oxygenation dynamics in the placenta. Segmentation of the time series can be used to derive T2* maps and perform whole-organ signal comparisons between differing population groups, thereby enabling quantitative analysis of placental function with the ultimate goal of developing biomarkers of placental and fetal health.

Acknowledgments. This work was supported in part by NIH NIBIB NAC P41EB015902, NIH NICHD R01HD100009, R01EB032708, R21HD106553, MIT-IBM Watson AI Lab, NSERC PGS D, NSF GRFP, and MathWorks Fellowship.

References

1. Abaci Turk, E., et al.: Placental MRI: effect of maternal position and uterine contractions on placental bold MRI measurements. Placenta **95**, 69–77 (2020)

2. Abaci Turk, E., et al.: Spatiotemporal alignment of in utero BOLD-MRI series. J. Magn. Reson. Imaging **46**(2), 403–412 (2017)
3. Abaci Turk, E., et al.: Placental MRI: developing accurate quantitative measures of oxygenation. Top. Magn. Reson. Imaging **28**(5), 285–297 (2019)
4. Abulnaga, S.M., Turk, E.A., Bessmeltsev, M., Grant, P.E., Solomon, J., Golland, P.: Volumetric parameterization of the placenta to a flattened template. IEEE Trans. Med. Imaging **41**(4), 925–936 (2022)
5. Alansary, A., et al.: Fast fully automatic segmentation of the human placenta from motion corrupted MRI. In: Ourselin, S., Joskowicz, L., Sabuncu, M.R., Unal, G., Wells, W. (eds.) MICCAI 2016. LNCS, vol. 9901, pp. 589–597. Springer, Cham (2016). https://doi.org/10.1007/978-3-319-46723-8_68
6. Lin, T.Y., Goyal, P., Girshick, R., He, K., Dollár, P.: Focal loss for dense object detection. In: 2017 IEEE International Conference on Computer Vision (ICCV), pp. 2999–3007 (2017)
7. Luo, J., et al.: In vivo quantification of placental insufficiency by BOLD MRI: a human study. Sci. Rep. **7**(1), 3713 (2017)
8. Miao, H., et al.: Placenta maps: in utero placental health assessment of the human fetus. IEEE Trans. Visual Comput. Graphics **23**(6), 1612–1623 (2017)
9. Milletari, F., Navab, N., Ahmadi, S.A.: V-net: fully convolutional neural networks for volumetric medical image segmentation. In: 2016 Fourth International Conference on 3D Vision (3DV), pp. 565–571 (2016)
10. Pietsch, M., et al.: APPLAUSE: automatic prediction of placental health via U-net segmentation and statistical evaluation. Med. Image Anal. **72**, 102145 (2021)
11. Pérez-García, F., Sparks, R., Ourselin, S.: TorchIO: a python library for efficient loading, preprocessing, augmentation and patch-based sampling of medical images in deep learning. Comput. Methods Programs Biomed. **208**, 106236 (2021)
12. Ronneberger, O., Fischer, P., Brox, T.: U-Net: convolutional networks for biomedical image segmentation. In: Navab, N., Hornegger, J., Wells, W.M., Frangi, A.F. (eds.) MICCAI 2015. LNCS, vol. 9351, pp. 234–241. Springer, Cham (2015). https://doi.org/10.1007/978-3-319-24574-4_28
13. Sinding, M., Peters, D.A., Frøkjær, J.B., Christiansen, O.B., Uldbjerg, N., Sørensen, A.: Reduced placental oxygenation during subclinical uterine contractions as assessed by BOLD MRI. Placenta **39**, 16–20 (2016)
14. Sinding, M., et al.: Placental baseline conditions modulate the hyperoxic BOLD-MRI response. Placenta **61**, 17–23 (2018)
15. Sørensen, A., et al.: Placental oxygen transport estimated by the hyperoxic placental BOLD MRI response. Physiol. Rep. **3**(10), e12582 (2015)
16. Sørensen, A., et al.: Changes in human fetal oxygenation during maternal hyperoxia as estimated by BOLD MRI. Prenat. Diagn. **33**(2), 141–145 (2013)
17. Specktor-Fadida, B., et al.: A bootstrap self-training method for sequence transfer: state-of-the-art placenta segmentation in fetal MRI. In: Sudre, C.H., et al. (eds.) UNSURE/PIPPI -2021. LNCS, vol. 12959, pp. 189–199. Springer, Cham (2021). https://doi.org/10.1007/978-3-030-87735-4_18
18. Steinweg, J.K., et al.: T2* placental MRI in pregnancies complicated with fetal congenital heart disease. Placenta **108**, 23–31 (2021)
19. Torrents-Barrena, J., et al.: Fully automatic 3D reconstruction of the placenta and its peripheral vasculature in intrauterine fetal MRI. Med. Image Anal. **54**, 263–279 (2019)
20. Torrents-Barrena, J., et al.: Segmentation and classification in MRI and US fetal imaging: recent trends and future prospects. Med. Image Anal. **51**, 61–88 (2019)

21. Uus, A., et al.: Deformable slice-to-volume registration for motion correction of fetal body and placenta MRI. IEEE Trans. Med. Imaging **39**(9), 2750–2759 (2020)

22. Wang, G., Li, W., Aertsen, M., Deprest, J., Ourselin, S., Vercauteren, T.: Aleatoric uncertainty estimation with test-time augmentation for medical image segmentation with convolutional neural networks. Neurocomputing **338**, 34–45 (2019)

23. Wang, G., et al.: Slic-Seg: slice-by-slice segmentation propagation of the placenta in fetal MRI using one-plane scribbles and online learning. In: Navab, N., Hornegger, J., Wells, W.M., Frangi, A.F. (eds.) MICCAI 2015. LNCS, vol. 9351, pp. 29–37. Springer, Cham (2015). https://doi.org/10.1007/978-3-319-24574-4_4

24. You, W., Andescavage, N.N., Kapse, K., Donofrio, M.T., Jacobs, M., Limperopoulos, C.: Hemodynamic responses of the placenta and brain to maternal hyperoxia in fetuses with congenital heart disease by using blood oxygen-level dependent MRI. Radiology **294**(1), 141–148 (2020)

25. You, W., Serag, A., Evangelou, I.E., Andescavage, N., Limperopoulos, C.: Robust motion correction and outlier rejection of in vivo functional MR images of the fetal brain and placenta during maternal hyperoxia. In: SPIE Medical Imaging, vol. 9417, pp. 177–189. SPIE (2015)

A Fast Anatomical and Quantitative MRI Fetal Exam at Low Field

Jordina Aviles[1,2(✉)], Kathleen Colford[1], Megan Hall[1,3], Massimo Marenzana[1],
Alena Uus[1,2], Sharon Giles[2], Philippa Bridgen[2], Mary A. Rutherford[1],
Shaihan J. Malik[1,2], Joseph V. Hajnal[1,2], Raphael Tomi-Tricot[2,4],
and Jana Hutter[1,2]

[1] Centre for the Developing Brain, School of Biomedical Engineering and Imaging
Sciences, King's College London, London, UK
jordina.aviles_verdera@kcl.ac.uk
[2] Department of Biomedical Engineering, School of Biomedical Engineering and
Imaging Sciences, King's College London, London, UK
[3] Department of Women and Children's Health, King's College London, London, UK
[4] MR Research Collaborations, Siemens Healthcare Limited, Camberley, UK

Abstract. Fetal Magnetic Resonance Imaging (Fetal MRI) allows
insights into human development before birth, complementing conven-
tional Ultrasound imaging with its high resolution and available numerous contrast options. Significant challenges still exist including geometric distortion caused by maternal bowel gas in echo-planar imaging, and
restrictions in bore size limiting access to MRI in the obese and or claustrophobic population. Recent developments of clinical low-field scanners
can meet these challenges and thus render fetal MRI more accessible.
This study shows anatomical imaging and quantitative T2* mapping
on a 0.55T system with an analysis pipeline for both placenta and
fetal brain. Results show an expected increased overall T2* compared
to higher fields, with values decreasing over gestation as shown at higher
field. Future work will be directed towards exploring additional types
of relaxometry and the use of the presented techniques in subjects with
higher Body Mass Index. Included data and analysis code are publicly
available.

Keywords: Fetal and Placental MRI · Low field

1 Introduction

Fetal Magnetic Resonance Imaging (MRI) is increasingly used for both research
and clinical fetal examinations. Its ability to offer high resolution, and both
anatomical and functional information allows fetal MRI to play a growing role in
perinatal management and early detection of pathologies complementing widely
used Ultrasound (US) screening. Multiple recent studies show an increasing range
of uses in fetal neurological applications [16], congenital heart disease, placental

R. Licandro et al. (Eds.): PIPPI 2022, LNCS 13575, pp. 13–24, 2022.
https://doi.org/10.1007/978-3-031-17117-8_2

pathologies such as placenta accreta, percreta and increta and in the prediction of pregnancy complications such as pre-eclampsia, fetal growth restriction and preterm birth. Thereby, two techniques have found particularly widespread use: First, T2-weighted anatomical imaging, often performed using single-shot 2D Turbo-Spin-Echo techniques to freeze fetal motion within each slice, is the standard for anatomical imaging due to its excellent soft tissue contrast and achievable high resolution. Typical assessments, which usually require motion correction, include fetal volumetric quantification of the fetal brain growth, the fetal body and the placenta. Second, more recently T2* relaxometry, sensitive to the concentration of deoxygenated haemoglobin via the blood-oxygen level dependency effect, has been more widely employed in a research capacity, especially to assess placental function [18].

A decreasing trend in placental mean T2* over gestational age has consistently been observed. Reduction in T2* has been shown in pregnancies associated with pre-eclampsia [10], fetal growth restriction and reduced birth weight [17] as well as congenital heart disease [19]. T2* data is typically acquired using a single shot gradient-echo Echo Planar Imaging (EPI) sequence acquired at different echo times (TE), either using repeated single-echo or multi-echo sequences.

Fetal MRI data is currently almost exclusively acquired at 1.5T and to a lesser extent 3T, with the move to ever higher field strength driven by the available higher signal-to-noise ratio (SNR) [15] allowing, for example, higher b-values for diffusion-weighted MRI, and thus the ability to probe smaller structures, as well as higher resolution anatomical scans. However, another recent emerging push in the opposite direction, towards lower field strengths, most notably for interventional applications, cardiac MRI and lung MRI, can be observed. The advantages of low field, such as reduced susceptibility to tissue-air interfaces, and thus reduced geometric distortions, often reduced bore length and wider diameter as well as longer T2* times, meet some of the requirements and challenges for fetal MRI: Reduced susceptibility lowers the requirements for shimming, typically required at high field targeted to the organ of interest [5] to reduce geometric distortions especially for functional EPI-based sequences. The increased comfort of the larger bore fits the requirements of an increasingly obese pregnant population and increases comfort for claustrophobic women of all sizes. Finally, the longer T2* times allow longer read-out trains to be employed in single-shot sequences and thus higher resolution.

First quantitative studies at 0.5T were presented in the late 90s by Gowland et al. in a purpose-built scanner, providing quantification of T1 and T2 in the human placenta from 20 weeks gestational age to term in both normal and compromised pregnancies [6]. Significant decay in T1 and T2 relaxation times with gestational age were shown for the first time in low-field. Furthermore, in compromised pregnancies with intra-uterine growth restriction and pre-eclampsia, T1 values were significant lower than in control group, this trend persisted for T2 but did not reach significance. These findings motivate the further exploration of low-field for pregnancy assessment and diagnostics.

Contributions

This work introduces a fast, 15 min fetal examination at 0.55T including full uterus anatomical and quantitative T2* imaging together with an analysis pipeline. It provides the first evidence of the feasibility of this approach at low field and initial data over gestation. Benefits and possible avenues to generate new information to be obtained at low field are discussed.

2 Methods

Pregnant women were scanned on a contemporary clinical 0.55T scanner (MAG-NETOM Free.Max, Siemens Healthcare, Erlangen, Germany) after informed consent was obtained as part of the MEERKAT study (REC 21/LO/0742). The acquisitions were performed with a 6-element flexible coil (BioMatrix Contour Coil, Siemens Healthcare, Erlangen, Germany) and a 9-element spine coil built in the patient table. Women were scanned in head first supine position fully supported with head and leg rests with continuous life monitoring including heart rate and blood pressure measurements as well as frequent verbal interaction. A mid examination break was offered but declined in all cases described here. Exclusion criteria were maintained from the high field studies and include maternal age < 16 years, lack of ability to consent, contraindications for MRI such as metal implants, claustrophobia, multiple pregnancies and a maximal weight of 200 kg.

Structural T2-weighted Turbo Spin Echo (TSE) acquisitions using the clinically available sequence was employed. For the T2* relaxometry, a clinical gradient echo single-shot EPI sequence was modified to include up to 5 back-to-back readout trains defining as many echoes.

The T2-weighted data sets were acquired in five different orientations, the parameters include resolution = $1.48 \times 1.48 \times 4.5\,\text{mm}^3$, FOV = $449 \times 499\,\text{mm}^2$ TE = 105–106 ms, TR = 1460–2500 ms and total acquisition time (TA) = 2 min–3 min. T2* acquisitions were performed in transverse orientation for the fetal brain and both transverse and coronal for the placenta. The quantitative T2* datasets were acquired with a resolution of $4\,\text{mm}^3$ isotropic and a FOV = $400 \times 400\,\text{mm}^2$, TEs = 80 ms, 222.62 ms and 365.24 ms, TR = 9670 ms, TA = 39 s. Parallel imaging for T2* was applied with same resolution and FOV, TEs = 44 ms, 117.92 ms and 191.84 ms, TR = 5120 ms and TA = 31 s. A 5 echoes image with parallel imaging with an acceleration factor of 2 was acquired for one of the patients. The T2 and T2* acquisitions were performed in a sequential order without global changes to the maternal position with a total acquisition time of 15 min.

In addition, to demonstrate the field-strength dependent differences, data sets with placental and brain T2* data acquired as part of another ethically approved study (REC 16/LO/1573) using a similar protocol on a clinical 3T scanner (Philips Achieva, 104 data sets) and on a clinical 1.5T scanner (Philips Ingenia, 50 data sets) were considered. This data was acquired following the same selection process as the present study, including only healthy volunteers with gestational age ranging from 16 to 40 weeks.

2.1 Evaluation

The included cohort consists of a total of eight datasets with gestational ages ranging from 21 to 37 weeks. Two of these subjects were diagnosed with high risk pregnancies. This included one with chronic hypertension and fetal growth restriction and another with threatened preterm labour and ruptured membranes. The remaining four were considered low risk controls, two of these were scanned twice during pregnancy, characteristics are given in Table 1.

Table 1. Studied cohort characteristics. cHTN: Chronic Hypertension; FGR: Fetal Growth Restriction; PPROM: Prolonged preterm rupture of the membranes. For the acquired data, a X in the third and/or fourth column indicates Turbo Spin Echo (TSE) data and/or gradient echo single-shot Echo-plannar Imaging (EPI) data was acquired.

Study ID	gestational age [weeks] at scan	Cohort	TSE data	EPI data
Participant 1	31.43	control	X	
Participant 2	30.28	control	X	
Participant 4	28.01	cHTN + FGR	X	
Participant 5	21.01	control		X
Participant 6	32.01	PPROM	X	X
Participant 1, scan 2	37.01	control	X	X
Participant 2, scan 2	33.85	control	X	X

2.2 Analysis

The obtained stack of TSE images of each subject at five different orientations was used as input dataset for a slice-to-volume (SVR) registration model by Uus et al. to generate motion-corrected fetal brain reconstructions (see Fig. 2) [21]. In parallel, a set of images (see Fig. 1) acquired at three to five different TEs were obtained from the single-shot multi-echo gradient echo sequences for both fetal brain and placentas of each subject. For the T2* fitting, 3D masks were obtained with open-source software either fully manually (placenta) or using manual refinement after automatic brain extraction was performed (brain). Quality of the segmentations was assessed by an expert radiographer (KC).

T2* values were obtained by fitting the signal intensity of each voxel within the placenta or brain as a function of echo time. Fitting was performed using a non-linear least squares regression in python of the following mono-exponential decay model:

$$S = M_0 \cdot e^{\frac{-TE_i}{T2^*}} \tag{1}$$

where M_0 is the proton density and TE_i contains the different echo times with $i \in [0, 5]$. M_0 was initialized with the voxel intensity at the first echo time and T2* initialization was in the range of 0–300 ms. Bounds range was 0–10000 for M_0, 0–500 ms for the T2* values in the placenta and 0–1000 ms for the fetal brain.

Fig. 1. Example of a placenta slice (top row) and fetal brain slice (bottom row) from 3D multi-echo gradient echo data across different TE (from left to right: 44 ms, 117.92 ms, 191.84 ms, 265.76 ms and 339.68 ms).

3   Results

Seven of the eight subjects tolerated the entire scan well, one woman was not comfortable and abandoned the scan after 10 min. T2w data is thus available for all but for that case, where not enough data was acquired for the SVR reconstruction. T2* scans were added in four of the eight subjects. Anatomical data from one of the cases is illustrated in Fig. 2, displaying a coronal and a sagittal view through the uterus as well as a resulting SVR result from the fetal brain.

Example multi-echo images from the placenta and brain with their corresponding T2* maps are shown in Fig. 3. Obtained T2* maps obtained have the capability to capture the differences in T2* between different regions of the fetal brain and highlight placental lobularity.

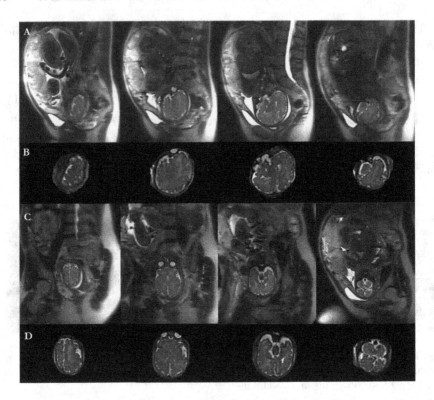

Fig. 2. Sagittal and coronal views of a structural T2-weighted TSE image at 37 weeks gestational age together with its corresponding SVR reconstruction of the fetal brain. A) Sagittal slices across the uterus; B) Sagittal slices of the fetal brain SVR; C) Coronal slices across the uterus together with D) the fetal brain SVR.

Figure 4 shows example data and the achieved fitted mono-exponential decay curves in the regions of interest (ROI) indicated. Two voxels in different regions of both placenta and fetal brain were selected and their intensities across TEs plotted. In the placenta, signal in the intervillous space is higher and decays slower than in the septa. Similar behaviour can be seen in the fetal brain fitting, where the voxel selected in the white matter region has higher values across the TEs than the one situated around the basal ganglia.

Mean T2* values across the fetal brain and placenta were calculated for each subject, together with brain and placenta volumes. Figure 5 shows these quantitative results in red over gestational age, superimposed over results from 3T (yellow) and 1.5T (violet) to allow cross-field strength comparison. Placental volume (A) shows a weak positive correlation with gestational age, independent of field strength. A clear negative correlation between mean placental T2* and gestational age can be observed on all field strength, with the absolute values of T2* increasing with field strength for similar gestational age (B). Mean T2* values obtained for the placenta are around 211 ms at around 21 weeks gestational age, dropping

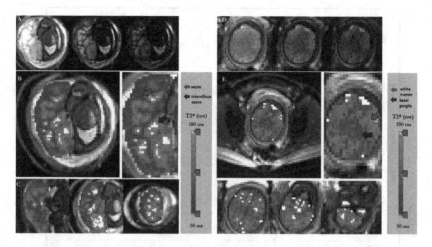

Fig. 3. Placenta and fetal brain gradient-echo images at 37 weeks gestational age over 3 echo times (from left to right: 44 ms, 117.92 ms, 191.84 ms) and their T2* maps over different axial slices. A) Slice of the placenta gradient-echo images over 3 TE; B) T2* map of the placenta overlaid on first echo time image in A and a zoom in with blue and green arrows pointing to the septa and intervillous space, respectively; C) Different placental T2* map slices over different axial views; D) Slice of the fetal brain gradient-echo images over 3 TE; E) T2* map of the fetal brain overlaid on first echo time image in B and a zoom in with blue and green arrows pointing to white matter and basal ganglia, respectively; F) Different fetal brain T2* map slices over different axial views; (Color figure online)

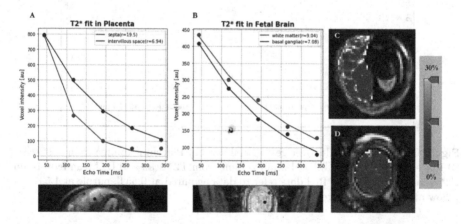

Fig. 4. T2* fitting in brain and placenta at 37 weeks gestational age examples with residual maps overlaid with the second echo image. A) T2* fitting for septa in blue and intervillous space in green on top with chosen voxels position on the bottom; B) T2* fitting for white matter in blue and basal ganglia in green on top with chosen voxels position on the bottom; C) Placenta residual map; D) Fetal Brain residual map with colormap on the right side. (Color figure online)

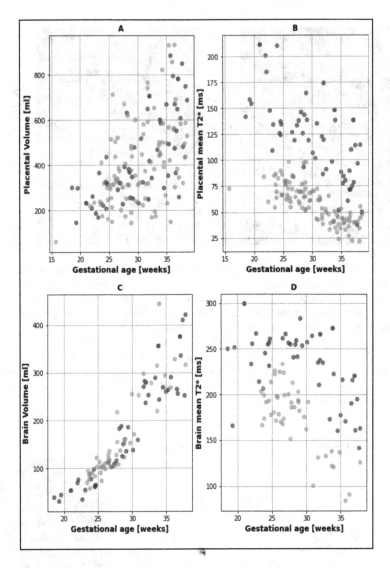

Fig. 5. Quantitative results over gestational age. A) Placental volume from T2* scan, B) Placental mean T2*, C) Fetal brain volume from T2* scan and D) Mean fetal brain T2* over gestational age. Red dots refer to data acquired at 0.55T, purple at 1.5T and yellow at 3T. (Color figure online)

to 107 ms at 37 weeks. A strong positive correlation can be observed between fetal brain volume and gestational age, again independent of field strength (C). Finally, a negative correlation between brain T2* and gestational age can be observed, with the data at the highest field strength (in yellow) again displaying the lowest overall values for the same gestational age and the data from low field (in red) on average with the highest values (D).

4   Discussion and Conclusions

The included dataset will be made available from the corresponding author upon reasonable academic request in accordance with the rules of ethical approval (REC 21/LO/0742). The analysis code is already available at Github Link. This work provides the important initial evidence of the feasibility of a short, clinically acceptable under 15 min anatomical and quantitative T2* analysis for low-field fetal MRI on a contemporary clinical low-field MRI.

It adds to the previous work by Gowland et al. in their purpose-built scanner [4,6–8], demonstrating the data quality achievable on a clinical scanner at this field strength. Despite its lower SNR, low-field MRI is known to be less susceptible to geometric distortion related to B0 inhomogeneities, translated here in achieving high quality data without using image based shimming techniques. Further studies will include B0 maps to quantitatively illustrate this. Wider bore diameters together with shorter length carry the potential to contribute to help with comfort and claustrophobia together with the possibility to scan pregnant women with higher BMI > 30.

Further studies will need to be performed to provide quantitative evidence for this. We show both anatomical data, suitable for high resolution reconstruction and T2* measurements in the brain and placenta. The achieved resolution for these functional scans allows robust identification of different brain and placental regions (Fig. 4, Fig. 3).

The achieved T2* maps are of good quality. Quantitative T2* results in this study are among the first reported, to the best of our knowledge, in an 0.55T scanner for fetal and placenta imaging. Matched T2* decay with gestational age with previously published studies, can be seen in both ROIs [1,11,18,22]. In agreement to previous work, Fig. 5 shows a clear decay in mean T2* values of the placenta with gestational age [11,12,18].

Following the same trend, fetal brain mean T2* also appears to decay with gestational age as previously reported by Vasylechko et al. [22]. The recorded fetal brain volume from these T2* scans is well in line with the volumes as obtained in other studies [2,3,13]. In addition, results obtained for total brain volume are aligned with the ones reported by Chang et al. over gestational age using Ultrasound fetal data [2].

While observing a decrease in T2* over gestational age, similar to all previous studies at 1.5T and 3T, the T2* values in this study are higher for same gestational age (211.19 ms at around 21 weeks gestational age compared to 120 ms on 1.5T and 75 at 3T) than previously reported on 1.5T or 3T, as expected [9,17]. These observed overall higher T2* times are in line with the general increase in T2* observed with decreasing field strength [14]. Figure 5 illustrates these trends for both placenta and brain in 0.55T, 1.5T and 3T.

The demonstrated higher T2* in the intervillous space, particularly close to the centers of the lobules and overall granularity illustrated is in agreement with previously published results [12]. The intervillous space receives inflowing maternal blood from the spiral arteries which continues along the villi to exchange oxygen and nutrients with the fetal blood. The oxygen-rich blood in this area, with increasing decay due to fetal uptake towards the borders of the lobules, is in line with the observed pattern. The vasculature in the septa on the other hand, carrying deoxygenated blood back to the maternal circulation corresponds well to the lower signal intensity. Notably, here at low field, the overall longer T2* times allow us to observe smaller differences in these low-signal regions even in later gestation (see Fig. 3 for a scan at 37 weeks).

Similar findings can be demonstrated in the fetal brain, where the basal ganglia show lower T2* than white matter in line with previous studies [22]. However, the reasons behind differences observed in the fetal brain remain unclear. Some studies suggest increased T2* is related to changes in myelin and iron concentration [22]. The observed higher T2* (see Fig. 5) in turn allows single-shot acquisitions with higher resolution, contributing to motion robustness and decreased loss in SNR compared to multi-shot sequences [20].

Obtained residual maps (see Fig. 4) show lower and more homogeneous results for the fetal brain than the placenta, where some anatomical relationship can be appreciated especially around the septa.

This preliminary study has, however, some limitations. The data set used included only a total of eight subjects with only four of them containing multi-echo EPI data. Although the results are in agreement with already published results in the field, a larger dataset with a wider spread across gestational age and including different placental and fetal brain pathologies is needed to further validate these results.

Another major limitation is fetal brain T2* were reported for the whole volume instead of differentiating between regions which might contribute to a better understanding of the clinical value of the parameter. Finally, although motion was assessed visually, no motion correction was applied in the multi-echo data, causing potential inconsistencies.

Future work will focus on including further modalities such as diffusion MRI, T1 relaxometry and perfusion MRI to study the developing placenta and fetus in even more detail. Moreover, taking advantage of low-field scanner properties, we will aim to include women with higher BMI to study the suitability of the proposed protocol to achieve good image quality in this challenging cohort. Finally, future studies will include a larger dataset, and explore the effect of motion correction on the present results.

Acknowledgments. The authors thank all the participating families as well as the midwives and radiographers involved in this study. This work was supported by the NIH (Human Placenta Project—grant 1U01HD087202-01), Wellcome Trust Sir Henry Wellcome Fellowship (201374/Z/16/Z and /B), UKRI FLF (MR/T018119/1), Wellcome-EPSRC Center for Medical Engineering, the NIHR Clinical Research Facility (CRF) at Guy's and St Thomas'. The views expressed are those of the authors and not necessarily those of the NHS or the NIHR.

References

1. Blazejewska, A.I., et al.: 3D in utero quantification of T2* relaxation times in human fetal brain tissues for age optimized structural and functional MRI. Magn. Reson. Med. **78**(3), 909–916 (2017)
2. Chang, C.H., Yu, C.H., Chang, F.M., Ko, H.C., Chen, H.Y.: The assessment of normal fetal brain volume by 3-D ultrasound. Ultrasound Med. Biol. **29**(9), 1267–1272 (2003)
3. Clouchoux, C., Guizard, N., Evans, A., Plessis, A.D., Limperopoulos, C.: Normative fetal brain growth by quantitative in vivo magnetic resonance imaging. Am. J. Obstet. Gynecol. **206**(2), 173-e1 (2012)
4. Fulford, J., et al.: Fetal brain activity in response to a visual stimulus. Hum. Brain Mapp. **20**(4), 239–245 (2003)
5. Gaspar, A.S., et al.: Optimizing maternal fat suppression with constrained image-based shimming in fetal MR. Magn. Reson. Med. **81**(1), 477–485 (2019)
6. Gowland, P.A., et al.: In vivo relaxation time measurements in the human placenta using echo planar imaging at 0.5 T. Magn. Reson. Imaging **16**(3), 241–247 (1998)
7. Gowland, P.: Placental MRI. Semin. Fetal Neonatal. Med. **10**(5), 485–490 (2005)
8. Gowland, P., Fulford, J.: Initial experiences of performing fetal fMRI. Exp. Neurol. **190**, 22–27 (2004)
9. Hansen, D.N., et al.: T2*-weighted placental magnetic resonance imaging: a biomarker of placental dysfunction in small-for-gestational-age pregnancies. Am. J. Obst. Gynecol. MFM **4**(3), 100578 (2022)
10. Ho, A.E.P., et al.: T2* placental magnetic resonance imaging in preterm preeclampsia: an observational cohort study. Hypertension **75**(6), 1523–1531 (2020)
11. Hutter, J., et al.: T2* relaxometry to characterize normal placental development over gestation in-vivo at 3T. Technical report, no. 4, p. 166. Wellcome Open Research (2019)
12. Hutter, J., et al.: Multi-modal functional MRI to explore placental function over gestation. Magn. Reson. Med. **81**(2), 1191–1204 (2019)
13. Kyriakopoulou, V., et al.: Normative biometry of the fetal brain using magnetic resonance imaging. Brain Struct. Funct. **222**(5), 2295–2307 (2017)
14. Marques, J.P., Simonis, F.F., Webb, A.G.: Low-field MRI: an MR physics perspective. J. Magn. Reson. Imaging **49**(6), 1528–1542 (2019)
15. Pohmann, R., Speck, O., Scheffler, K.: Signal-to-noise ratio and MR tissue parameters in human brain imaging at 3, 7, and 9.4 tesla using current receive coil arrays. Magn. Reson. Med. **75**(2), 801–809 (2016). https://doi.org/10.1002/mrm.25677
16. Rajagopalan, V., Deoni, S., Panigrahy, A., Thomason, M.E.: Is fetal MRI ready for neuroimaging prime time? An examination of progress and remaining areas for development. Dev. Cogn. Neurosci. **51**, 100999 (2021)
17. Sinding, M., et al.: Placental magnetic resonance imaging T2* measurements in normal pregnancies and in those complicated by fetal growth restriction. Ultrasound Obstet. Gynecol. **47**(6), 748–754 (2016)
18. Sorensen, A.V., Hutter, J.M., Grant, E.P., Seed, M., Gowland, P.: T2* weighted Placental MRI: basic research tool or an emerging clinical test of placental dysfunction? Ultrasound Obstet. Gynecol. (2019)
19. Steinweg, J.K., et al.: T2* placental MRI in pregnancies complicated with fetal congenital heart disease. Placenta **108**, 23–31 (2021) https://doi.org/10.1016/j.placenta.2021.02.015. https://www.sciencedirect.com/science/article/pii/S0143400421000680

20. Swisher, J.D., Sexton, J.A., Gatenby, J.C., Gore, J.C., Tong, F.: Multishot versus single-shot pulse sequences in very high field fMRI: a comparison using retinotopic mapping. PLoS ONE **7**(4), e34626 (2012)
21. Uus, A., et al.: Deformable slice-to-volume registration for motion correction in fetal body MRI. IEEE TMI **39**(9), 2750–2759 (2020). arXiv:1906.08827
22. Vasylechko, S.: Motion robust acquisition and reconstruction of quantitative T2* maps in the developing brain (2019)

Automatic Fetal Fat Quantification from MRI

Netanell Avisdris[1,2]([✉]) [iD], Aviad Rabinowich[2,3,4], Daniel Fridkin[1],
Ayala Zilberman[4,5], Sapir Lazar[3,4], Jacky Herzlich[4,6], Zeev Hananis[2],
Daphna Link-Sourani[4], Liat Ben-Sira[3,4], Liran Hiersch[4,5],
Dafna Ben Bashat[2,4,7], and Leo Joskowicz[1]

[1] School of Computer Science and Engineering,
The Hebrew University of Jerusalem, Jerusalem, Israel
{netana03,josko}@cs.huji.ac.il
[2] Sagol Brain Institute, Tel Aviv Sourasky Medical Center, Tel Aviv, Israel
[3] Department of Radiology, Tel Aviv Medical Center, Tel Aviv, Israel
[4] Sackler Faculty of Medicine, Tel Aviv University, Tel Aviv, Israel
[5] Department of Obstetrics and Gynecology, Lis Hospital for Women,
Tel Aviv Sourasky Medical Center, Tel Aviv, Israel
[6] Neonatal Intensive Care Unit, Dana Dwek Children's Hospital,
Tel Aviv Sourasky Medical Center, Tel Aviv, Israel
[7] Sagol School of Neuroscience, Tel Aviv University, Tel Aviv, Israel

Abstract. Normal fetal adipose tissue (AT) development is essential
for perinatal well-being. AT, or simply fat, stores energy in the form
of lipids. Malnourishment may result in excessive or depleted adiposity.
Although previous studies showed a correlation between the amount of
AT and perinatal outcome, prenatal assessment of AT is limited by lack-
ing quantitative methods. Using magnetic resonance imaging (MRI), 3D
fat- and water-only images of the entire fetus can be obtained from two-
point Dixon images to enable AT lipid quantification. This paper is the
first to present a methodology for developing a deep learning (DL) based
method for fetal fat segmentation based on Dixon MRI. It optimizes radiologists' manual fetal fat delineation time to produce annotated training
dataset. It consists of two steps: 1) model-based semi-automatic fetal
fat segmentations, reviewed and corrected by a radiologist; 2) automatic fetal fat segmentation using DL networks trained on the resulting annotated dataset. Segmentation of 51 fetuses was performed with
the semi-automatic method. Three DL networks were trained. We show
a significant improvement in segmentation times (3:38 h → <1 h) and
observer variability (Dice of 0.738 → 0.906) compared to manual segmentation. Automatic segmentation of 24 test cases with the 3D Residual U-Net, nn-UNet and SWIN-UNetR transformer networks yields a
mean Dice score of 0.863, 0.787 and 0.856, respectively. These results
are better than the manual observer variability, and comparable to automatic adult and pediatric fat segmentation. A Radiologist reviewed and
corrected six new independent cases segmented using the best performing network (3D Residual U-Net), resulting in a Dice score of 0.961 and
a significantly reduced correction time of 15:20 min. Using these novel

R. Licandro et al. (Eds.): PIPPI 2022, LNCS 13575, pp. 25–37, 2022.
https://doi.org/10.1007/978-3-031-17117-8_3

segmentation methods and short MRI acquisition time, whole body subcutaneous lipids can be quantified for individual fetuses in the clinic and large-cohort research.

Keywords: Fetal adipose tissue · Fetal MRI · Automatic segmentation

1   Introduction

The adipose tissue (AT) is essential for fetal development and reflects the overall fetal energy balance. AT, or simply fat, stores energy in the form of lipids. Typically, well-nourished fetuses show an accelerated AT growth from the 28 weeks of gestation onward [20]. Although birth weight is often used as a proxy of fetal nutrition and as a predictor of adverse perinatal outcome, prior studies suggest that fetal body fat may show high correlation and be better predictor for neonatal outcomes [1,4,27]. Previous studies using ultrasound (US) showed alternations of fetal AT related to fetal growth restriction and excess of fetal AT in cases of maternal diabetes [11,18,25]. Furthermore, these changes also correlate with neonatal outcomes, emphasizing the clinical relevance of AT quantification. Although US is the method of choice for fetal development assessment, it is limited by the lack of true 3D information. Thus, fat estimation currently relies on linear and area measurements of selected fetal body parts, e.g., the abdomen and the limbs, and on estimated fractional limb volume [19], with no full body AT fat content volume quantification and analysis.

Magnetic resonance imaging (MRI) provides 3D multi-contrast information that indirectly characterizes the microstructural properties of tissue. For fat assessment, the two-point Dixon method [8], a proton chemical shift MRI technique that produces separated fat-only and water-only images from a dual-echo acquisition, is used. In this method, water and fat signals alternate between being summed and subtracted, yielding fat-only and water-only images that can be analyzed to quantify lipids. This method is used to quantify the lipid content of various organs, most extensively for hepatosteatosis assessment [13].

Fetal MRI is increasingly used as a complementary method to US, mainly for detecting central nervous system (CNS) and non-CNS anomalies, including thoracic, gastrointestinal, genitourinary, and skeletal anomalies [5]. A few studies measured AT of fetuses with normal-growth and with maternal diabetes [2,3,12]. However, these studies are limited, as they rely on linear measurements [2], on local assessment [3], or require laborious manual segmentation [12].

Automatic 3D MRI segmentation can enable accurate and reliable routine AT lipid quantification. Recently, deep learning (DL) based models have been increasingly used for automated segmentation of structures in medical imaging, including fetal structures [23,29]. While most methods address fetal brain segmentation, a few have been developed for other fetal structures and organs.

To the best of our knowledge, no automatic or semi-automatic methods for fetal fat quantification in US or MRI have been developed. Roelants et al. [24] described automated methods for US limb soft-tissue quantification, a surrogate for subcutaneous AT lipid deposition. Mack et al. [22] presented a semi-automatic method for fractional limb volume assessment and showed that it reduces observer variability and annotation time. Recent papers described automatic DL methods for fat segmentation in Dixon scans of adults in the pancreas [21] and visceral and subcutaneous fat [10,17]. Estrada et al. [10] reported that manual fat delineation is tedious and time-consuming, thus limiting its clinical and research applications. Fat segmentation poses several significant challenges compared to other structures. First, ground-truth manual fetal fat delineations are time-consuming, laborious and difficult to acquire [10,12], and suffer from high observer variability [15]. Indeed, fat structure is thin and complex, is distributed in various locations, and may appear as multiple disjoint components with a wide variety of shapes. Moreover, Dixon scans exhibit inherent limitations, e.g., signal inhomogeneity, artifacts due to high sensitivity to fetal and maternal motion, and obscured lipid-poor tissues in fat-only images, which lack the fetus context without the water-only images and requires additional MRI sequences.

In this paper, we present a methodology for creating the first reported automatic DL-based method for fetal fat segmentation on Dixon images. Its contributions are three-fold: (1) a semi-automatic segmentation method for fetal fat delineation that substantially shortens the manual annotation time and reduces inter-observer variability; (2) training and evaluation of three state-of-the-art deep learning models for fetal fat segmentation on the validated ground-truth segmentations generated by the semi-automatic method; (3) quantification of the manual and semi-automatic delineation observer variability and annotation time of fetal fat.

2   Methodology

Our methodology for fetal fat segmentation consists of: 1) semi-automatic fetal fat model-based segmentation whose aim is to shorten the manual fetal fat delineation time required to produce annotated training data, and; 2) automatic fetal fat segmentation with DL networks trained on the resulting annotated dataset.

2.1   Semi-automatic Fetal AT Segmentation

The inputs for the semi-automatic fetal fat segmentation method are two MRI sequences, fetal body TRUFI and fat-only Dixon, and the output is an initial subcutaneous fetal fat segmentation on the Dixon scan (Fig. 1). The TRUFI sequence is used to obtain fetal body segmentation that defines the Volume of Interest (VOI) in the Dixon scan on which the fetal fat segmentation is computed. Although the TRUFI and Dixon scans are acquired at subsequent times, they have different field-of-views and may not be aligned due to fetal and maternal motion.

First, the fetal body is automatically segmented on the TRUFI scan with the DL model described in [9]. The resulting segmentation mask is then mapped to the Dixon scan using the scanning position information to define a VOI that includes the entire fetus and excludes the maternal abdominal fat regions.

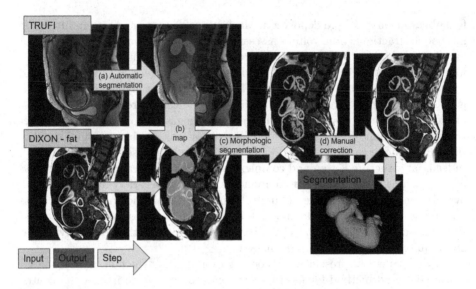

Fig. 1. Semi-automatic fetal fat segmentation method. The inputs (light blue) are fetal body TRUFI and fat-only Dixon scan. The four steps (grey arrows) of the method are: (a) automatic segmentation of the fetal body in the TRUFI scans; (b) mapping of the resulting segmentation as a VOI on the fat-only Dixon volume; (c) automatic segmentation of the fetal fat on the Dixon scan by thresholding and morphology operations; (d) revision and manual correction by a radiologist of the resulting fetal fat segmentation mask on each slice. The output (green) is a validated fetal fat segmentation mask. (Color figure online)

Manual adjustments to the resulting VOI are performed as required. The fetal fat within the VOI is then thresholded with a pre-defined value chosen experimentally. Connected components with <50 voxels are discarded to remove artifacts with similar fat intensity. The result is then reviewed and corrected by an expert radiologist to produce high-quality, validated ground truth segmentation masks.

2.2 Automatic Fetal Fat Segmentation

Automatic fetal fat segmentation is performed with a state-of-the-art DL model trained on the high-quality annotations of the fetal fat created in the previous step. The inputs are fat-only and water-only Dixon volumes, which are acquired simultaneously, and are thus aligned. The output is the fetal fat segmentation (Fig. 2).

We evaluate three models: (1) Residual 3D U-Net [16]; (2) nn-UNet [14], and; (3) SWIN-UNetR [28]. The 3D U-Net and nn-UNet are fully convolutional (FCN) encoder-decoder networks, where the decoder network is connected to the encoder network through skip connections. SWIN-UNetR is a combined transformer-FCN network. We briefly describe them next.

Residual 3D U-Net is a 3D-UNet [6] in which the encoder and decoder network blocks are residual units. 3D U-Net is a FCN which consists of a contraction path and an expansion path. The contraction path is an encoder that captures

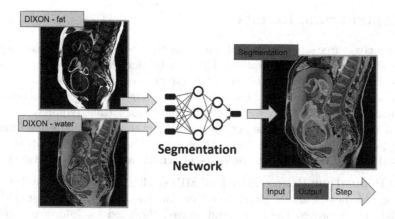

Fig. 2. Automatic fetal fat segmentation. The inputs (light blue) are fat-only and water-only Dixon scans. The output (green) is the fetal fat segmentation with a DL network. (Color figure online)

the context, while the expansion path is a decoder network that performs up-sampling to recover the segmentation map size. The encoder and decoder paths are connected through skip connections to share localization information.

nn-UNet is a biomedical image segmentation framework that automatically adapts to a dataset characteristics. It selects a segmentation network from a wide range of options, including 2D- and 3D- U-Net, and configures their hyper-parameters, e.g., patch size, batch size, or learning rate. It achieves state-of-the-art results on a wide range of biomedical image segmentation scenarios.

Transformers are new DL architectures that achieved state-of-the-art results in a wide range of machine learning tasks, including medical imaging [26]. Shifted windows (SWIN) Transformers is a hierarchical vision transformer that allows for local computing of self-attention with non-overlapping windows. SWIN is more efficient than regular vision transformers and is well-suited for tasks requiring multi-scale modeling due to its hierarchical nature. **SWIN-UNetR** is a vision transformer for biomedical image analysis. It consists of a SWIN transformer as the encoder and a CNN-based decoder. SWIN-UNetR computes self-attention in an efficient shifted window partitioning scheme. It is currently the best performing model on wide-varied biomedical image segmentation tasks.

Implementation Details: The 3D-UNet and SWIN-UNetR models were implemented in MONAI [7]; nn-UNet was implemented in Pytorch. All networks were trained on $128 \times 128 \times 128$ patches for 300 epochs on a single NVIDIA V100 GPU. 3D-UNet was trained with an ADAM optimizer with an initial learning rate of 1×10^{-2} and batch size of 10. SWIN-UNetR was trained with an AdamW optimizer with a warm-up cosine scheduler of 50 iterations and batch size of 1 patch. Both 3D-UNet and SWIN-UNetR are trained with random patch cropping and Gaussian noise augmentations, with Dice loss. Since nn-UNet is an automated framework, no training hyper-parameters were selected. For inference, we use a sliding window with an overlap of 0.7 for neighboring voxels.

3   Experimental Results

We conducted three studies. Study 1 quantifies the observer variability of manual and semi-automatic fat delineation. The manual delineation observer variability provides a reference for the expected target accuracy; the semi-automatic delineation observer variability quantifies the expected improvement in observer agreement. The study also measures the radiologist time required for each method. Study 2 quantifies the performance of the three automatic DL fetal fat segmentation methods. Study 3 quantifies and analyze the segmentation accuracy and correction time using the best-performing automatic DL network.

Study Population: Retrospective fetal MRI studies were collected at Tel Aviv Sourasky Medical Center, Israel, between 2019 and 2022. The institutional review board approved the study and waived the need for informed consent. The dataset consisted of 57 singleton fetuses ranging between 31 and 39+1 gestation weeks (mean = 33.9, std = 1.8). Participants were referred to fetal MRI for various clinical indications. Cases with chromosomal or congenital anomalies were excluded.

Data Acquisition and Ground Truth Generation: Patients were scanned on one of three 3T MRI scanners (Skyra, Prisma and Vida, Siemens Healthineers). Two subsequent sequences were used for this study: (a) free-breathing T2-weighted TRUFI sequence with voxel resolution of $0.78 \times 0.78 \times 2 \, \text{mm}^3$ and an acquisition time of 60 s, and (b) two-point Dixon sequence with voxel resolution of $1.25 - 1.4 \times 1.25 - 1.4 \times 1.5 - 2 \, \text{mm}^3$. The Dixon sequence was acquired with a single breath-hold, with acquisition time of 18–20 s. ITK-SNAP(v. 3.8.0) [30] was used for manual delineation and segmentation correction.

Evaluation Metrics: Five metrics were used to estimate observer agreement and evaluate segmentation methods: Dice similarity coefficient, Hausdorff distance, Average Symmetric Surface Distance (ASSD), volume difference (VD), and relative volume difference (RVD). RVD is defined as the VD divided by the fetal body volume. We used a two-sided t-test to estimate statistical significance, $p < 0.05$ was considered significant.

3.1   Study 1: Manual and Semi-automatic Observer Variability

No previous study has analyzed the inter-observer variability in fetal fat segmentation. Manual and semi-automatic segmentations were assessed by two radiologists that were blinded to study indication and gestational age. A previous study noted extremely long manual segmentation times [12]. Therefore, four consecutive slices on 10 scans were randomly selected for manual segmentation in the fetal volume. For the semi-automatic segmentation, the first observer (R1) segmented the entire cohort. Ten cases were assigned to a second independent observer (R2) to establish a baseline for the automatic method and to assess the segmentation quality. Manual delineation and correction times were recorded.

Table 1 lists the results. Overall, manual fat segmentation was very time-consuming, with a mean of 3:38 h (R1: 3:43 h, R2: 3:34 h) for the entire fat fetal volume, similar to the reported time in [12]. Semi-automatic segmentation significantly reduced total segmentation time to a mean of 0:57 h ($p = 6.3 \times 10^{-7}$). Furthermore, semi-automatic delineation significantly increased the inter-observer agreement for Dice and RVD: Dice increased by 0.186 ($p = 3 \times 10^{-5}$). Also, Hausdorff decreased by 4.20 mm ($p = 0.585$), ASSD decreased by 1.54 mm ($p = 0.228$) and RVD decreased by 20.55% ($p = 3 \times 10^{-5}$).

Table 1. Inter-observer variability of fetal fat delineation between two radiologists using two methods: manual and semi-automatic. Bold face indicates best results for each of the five metrics.

	Manual				Semi-automatic			
	mean	std	min	max	mean	std	min	max
Dice	0.738	0.092	0.567	0.865	**0.906**	**0.084**	0.744	0.981
Hausdorff [mm]	21.09	24.66	2.24	86.82	**16.88**	**5.10**	10.44	28.32
ASSD [mm]	1.90	4.11	0.23	13.57	**0.36**	**0.28**	0.07	0.87
VD [mL]	-	-	-	-	18.69	20.63	2.50	73.48
RVD [%]	29.91	12.54	6.26	46.34	**9.26**	**9.14**	1.10	26.50

3.2   Study 2: Automatic Fetal AT Segmentation

We evaluate three networks for the automatic fetal AT segmentation task: 3D Residual U-Net, nn-UNet, and SWIN-UNetR. A dataset of 51 manually corrected volumes from semi-automatic fetal fat segmentation was used. The networks were trained on 21 volumes; six volumes were used for validation and hyper-parameter choice. The networks were tested on an independent set of 24 volumes. Results are listed on Table 2. Overall, 3D Residual UNet yielded the best results, achieving an average Dice score of 0.862, above the manual delineation observer variability. Figure 3 shows illustrative fetal fat segmentation results of three fetuses.

Table 2. Study 2 results: comparison of three networks for fetal AT segmentation: 3D Residual UNet, nn-UNet and SWIN-UNetR on test-set (n=24). Bold face indicates best results for a metric.

	3D Residual UNet				nn-UNet				SWIN-UNetR			
	mean	std	min	max	mean	std	min	max	mean	std	min	max
Dice	**0.862**	**0.063**	0.609	0.926	0.787	0.169	0.269	0.927	0.856	0.082	0.538	0.933
Hausdorff [mm]	**18.05**	**4.88**	9.70	28.58	37.19	34.06	9.43	134.85	20.63	5.74	9.17	36.07
ASSD [mm]	**0.60**	**0.33**	0.30	1.93	1.54	2.09	0.32	7.52	0.66	0.51	0.25	2.78
VD [mL]	**16.93**	27.16	0.74	138.38	27.67	36.08	1.53	177.89	19.45	38.47	0.19	189.00
RVD [%]	**7.11**	**7.44**	0.50	36.66	13.59	15.78	0.82	71.60	8.36	11.50	0.12	50.07

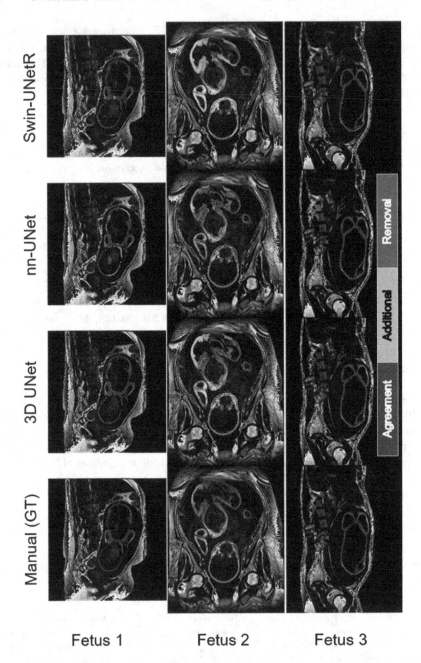

Fig. 3. Comparison of automatic segmentation networks performance. Three examples (columns) of manual ground-truth and three automatic segmentation networks (rows). The manual and automatic agreement voxels are represented in blue, green indicates under-segmentation voxels, and red indicates over segmentation voxels. nn-UNet tends to have over-segmented components, including large out-of-fetus components (e.g. in Fetus 3). (Color figure online)

3.3   Study 3: Analysis of Manual Corrections Following Automatic Segmentation

In order to evaluate the automatic method's effectiveness, six additional test cases were segmented using the best performing network, 3D Residual UNet. Following the automatic segmentation, cases were manually corrected by a radiologist (R1), and manual correction times were recorded.

Table 3. Study 3 results. Manual correction on best performing automatic segmentation network (3D Residual UNet) for 6 cases.

	mean	std	min	max
Dice	0.961	0.025	0.915	0.983
Hausdorff [mm]	48.72	29.67	13.08	84.30
ASSD [mm]	0.59	1.00	0.10	2.63
VD [mL]	7.54	10.91	1.62	29.35
RVD [%]	4.68	5.48	1.37	15.56

Results are listed in Table 3. Overall, only minor revisions were required (Dice of 0.961), and correction times were reduced to an average of 15:20 min. However, the Hausdorff distance was relatively high, 48.72 mm, compared to the inter-observer one (16.88 mm). Visual examples of corrections are presented in Fig. 4. Note that minor corrections were performed on small, out-of-fetus voxels (yellow arrow on Fig. 4), which may explain this result. Additional corrections were performed on lipid-poor areas such as the scalp, intensity artifacts, and non-subcutaneous fat depots (e.g., perirenal fat). All fetus body parts were segmented using the automatic method, with only minor voxels difference, resulting in a relatively small RVD of 4.68%.

4   Discussion

In this paper, we describe methods for semi-automatic and automatic fetal sub-cutaneous fat segmentation. We propose a semi-automatic segmentation method to delineate the fetal subcutaneous fat and showed that it significantly improves segmentation times and observer variability compared to manual segmentation. We then used the resulting segmentation masks to train an automatic deep-learning network, which yields accurate results, better than the inter-observer variability on manual segmentation, and shorten the correction time.

Automatic fat segmentation, and specifically fetal fat segmentation, is known to be a very challenging task. Previous works suggest that segmentation observer variability can be used as a surrogate to estimate the expected accuracy of automatic segmentation [15]. Here we show that fetal subcutaneous fat delineation has a high inter-observer variability with a Dice of 0.738 vs. 0.85–0.95 typically

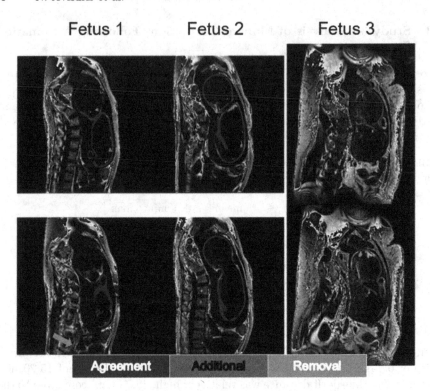

Fig. 4. Examples of manual correction on best performing automatic segmentation network (3D Residual UNet) of three fetuses (columns) from two representative slices (rows). The yellow arrow points to a small out-of-fetus segmented compartment that needs to be erased. (Color figure online)

observed for other fetal structures [29], which may be correlated to the difficulty of automatic segmentation. Estrada et al. [10] report an inter-observer variability of 0.982 and 0.788 Dice scores for adult subcutaneous and visceral fat, respectively. Adult visceral fat segmentation problem is similar to that of fetal subcutaneous fat, as it is a complex, sparse structure with many connected components, due to the intestines and the large surface it covers.

To address these issues, we used a semi-automatic method that reduced the observer variability and shorten segmentation times. These results suggest the advantage of using a semi-automatic segmentation to more efficiently produce more accurate ground-truth annotations used to train an automatic DL method. This scheme is similar to the one described in Kway et al. [17] for pediatric subcutaneous and visceral fat segmentations.

In this work, we explore the use of three neural networks for fetal fat segmentation. In particular, we compare the state-of-the-art models Residual 3D UNet, nn-UNet [14] and SWIN-UNetR [28]. In previous works [10,17], variants of 3D-UNet were used to automate fat segmentation. However, nn-UNet and SWIN-UNetR, which yield state-of-the-art results in a variety of biomedical image segmentation scenarios were not evaluated on fat segmentation tasks. In our study, SWIN-UNetR and 3D-UNet achieved similar results, while nn-UNet performed poorly. A possible explanation might relate to the different characteristics of fat segmentation, which differ from what nn-UNet was designed for [14]. Related fat segmentation methods achieved a Dice of 0.850 and 0.872 for pediatric and adults, respectively [10,17]. Our result of 0.862 is comparable to those results, and is better than observer variability of manual delineation. Moreover, the automatic method achieved an RVD of 7.11%, which is lower than the inter-observer variability RVD of 29.91% (manual) and 9.26% (semi-automatic).

Our study have several limitations. First, this is a single center cohort, which may result in poor generalization. Second, we include fetuses with a gestation age of 31 weeks or more, which may limit the automatic segmentation for younger fetuses. However, previous studies showed that the fetal fat is apparent in MRI only from the 28th week with rapid third trimester lipid accumulation [3,12]. Therefore, the pivotal age for fat quantification is similar to that of our study. Third, our cohort size of 57 fetuses is relatively small. Future studies should use a larger, and wider gestational age range to develop and assess the applicability of automatic methods for fetal fat quantification. Lastly, we explored the naive use of state-of-the-art DL methods. Future studies may design a more targeted solution of DL method in order to further improve fetal fat automatic segmentation and reduce the need for manual correction.

5 Conclusion

Here we propose the first method to automate subcutaneous fetal fat segmentation. We show that using state-of-the-art segmentation methods and short acquisition time MRI sequences, whole fetal body subcutaneous lipids can be quantified. We anticipate that our method can be used to study normal changes of fetal fat with gestational age and its relation to various abnormal conditions, e.g., gestational diabetes and fetal growth restriction.

Acknowledgements. This research was supported by Kamin Grants [63418, 72126] from the Israel Innovation Authority.

References

1. Banting, S.A., et al.: Estimation of neonatal body fat percentage predicts neonatal hypothermia better than birthweight centile. J. Matern.-Fetal Neonatal Med. 1–8 (2022)
2. Berger-Kulemann, V., et al.: Quantification of the subcutaneous fat layer with MRI in fetuses of healthy mothers with no underlying metabolic disease vs. fetuses of diabetic and obese mothers. J. Perinat. Med. (2012)
3. Blondiaux, E., et al.: Developmental patterns of fetal fat and corresponding signal on T1-weighted magnetic resonance imaging. Pediatr. Radiol. **48**(3), 317–324 (2018)

4. Carberry, A.E., Raynes-Greenow, C.H., Turner, R.M., Askie, L.M., Jeffery, H.E.: Is body fat percentage a better measure of undernutrition in newborns than birth weight percentiles? Pediatr. Res. **74**(6), 730–736 (2013)
5. Cassart, M., Garel, C.: European overview of current practice of fetal imaging by pediatric radiologists: a new task force is launched. Pediatr. Radiol. **50**(12), 1794–1798 (2020)
6. Çiçek, Ö., Abdulkadir, A., Lienkamp, S.S., Brox, T., Ronneberger, O.: 3D U-Net: learning dense volumetric segmentation from sparse annotation. In: Ourselin, S., Joskowicz, L., Sabuncu, M.R., Unal, G., Wells, W. (eds.) MICCAI 2016. LNCS, vol. 9901, pp. 424–432. Springer, Cham (2016). https://doi.org/10.1007/978-3-319-46723-8_49
7. MONAI Consortium: MONAI: medical open network for AI (2022). https://doi.org/10.5281/zenodo.6639453
8. Dixon, W.T.: Simple proton spectroscopic imaging. Radiology **153**(1), 189–194 (1984)
9. Dudovitch, G., Link-Sourani, D., Ben Sira, L., Miller, E., Ben Bashat, D., Joskowicz, L.: Deep learning automatic fetal structures segmentation in MRI scans with few annotated datasets. In: Martel, A.L., et al. (eds.) MICCAI 2020. LNCS, vol. 12266, pp. 365–374. Springer, Cham (2020). https://doi.org/10.1007/978-3-030-59725-2_35
10. Estrada, S., et al.: FatSegNet: a fully automated deep learning pipeline for adipose tissue segmentation on abdominal Dixon MRI. Magn. Reson. Med. **83**(4), 1471–1483 (2020)
11. Gardeil, F., Greene, R., Stuart, B., Turner, M.J.: Subcutaneous fat in the fetal abdomen as a predictor of growth restriction. Obstet. Gynecol. **94**(2), 209–212 (1999)
12. Giza, S.A., et al.: Water-fat magnetic resonance imaging of adipose tissue compartments in the normal third trimester fetus. Pediatr. Radiol. **51**(7), 1214–1222 (2021)
13. Hu, H.H., et al.: Linearity and bias of proton density fat fraction as a quantitative imaging biomarker: a multicenter, multiplatform, multivendor phantom study. Radiology **298**(3), 640 (2021)
14. Isensee, F., Jaeger, P.F., Kohl, S.A., Petersen, J., Maier-Hein, K.H.: nnU-Net: a self-configuring method for deep learning-based biomedical image segmentation. Nat. Methods **18**(2), 203–211 (2021)
15. Joskowicz, L., Cohen, D., Caplan, N., Sosna, J.: Inter-observer variability of manual contour delineation of structures in CT. Eur. Radiol. **29**(3), 1391–1399 (2019)
16. Kerfoot, E., Clough, J., Oksuz, I., Lee, J., King, A.P., Schnabel, J.A.: Left-ventricle quantification using residual U-Net. In: Pop, M., et al. (eds.) STACOM 2018. LNCS, vol. 11395, pp. 371–380. Springer, Cham (2019). https://doi.org/10.1007/978-3-030-12029-0_40
17. Kway, Y.M., et al.: Automated segmentation of visceral, deep subcutaneous, and superficial subcutaneous adipose tissue volumes in MRI of neonates and young children. Radiol. Artif. Intell. **3**(5) (2021)
18. Larciprete, G., et al.: Intrauterine growth restriction and fetal body composition. Ultrasound Obstet. Gynecol. **26**(3), 258–262 (2005)
19. Lee, W., et al.: New fetal weight estimation models using fractional limb volume. Ultrasound Obstet. Gynecol. **34**(5), 556–565 (2009)
20. Lee, W., et al.: The fetal arm: individualized growth assessment in normal pregnancies. J. Ultrasound Med. **24**(6), 817–828 (2005)

21. Lin, D., et al.: Automated measurement of pancreatic fat deposition on Dixon MRI using nnU-Net. J. Magn. Reson. Imaging (2022)
22. Mack, L.M., Kim, S.Y., Lee, S., Sangi-Haghpeykar, H., Lee, W.: A novel semiautomated fractional limb volume tool for rapid and reproducible fetal soft tissue assessment. J. Ultrasound Med. **35**(7), 1573–1578 (2016)
23. Meshaka, R., Gaunt, T., Shelmerdine, S.C.: Artificial intelligence applied to fetal MRI: a scoping review of current research. Br. J. Radiol. **95**, 20211205 (2022)
24. Roelants, J., et al.: Foetal fractional thigh volume: an early 3D ultrasound marker of neonatal adiposity. Pediatr. Obes. **12**, 65–71 (2017)
25. Nobile de Santis, M., et al.: Growth of fetal lean mass and fetal fat mass in gestational diabetes. Ultrasound Obstet. Gynecol. **36**(3), 328–337 (2010)
26. Shamshad, F., et al.: Transformers in medical imaging: a survey. arXiv preprint arXiv:2201.09873 (2022)
27. Shaw, M., Lutz, T., Gordon, A.: Does low body fat percentage in neonates greater than the 5th percentile birthweight increase the risk of hypoglycaemia and neonatal morbidity? J. Paediatr. Child Health **55**(12), 1424–1428 (2019)
28. Tang, Y., et al.: Self-supervised pre-training of swin transformers for 3D medical image analysis. In: Proceedings of IEEE Computer Society Conference on Computer Vision and Pattern Recognition, pp. 20730–20740 (2022)
29. Torrents-Barrena, J., et al.: Segmentation and classification in MRI and us fetal imaging: recent trends and future prospects. Med. Image Anal. **51**, 61–88 (2019)
30. Yushkevich, P.A., Gao, Y., Gerig, G.: ITK-SNAP: an interactive tool for semiautomatic segmentation of multi-modality biomedical images. In: International Conference of IEEE Engineering in Medicine and Biology Society (2016)

Continuous Longitudinal Fetus Brain Atlas Construction via Implicit Neural Representation

Lixuan Chen[1], Jiangjie Wu[1], Qing Wu[1], Hongjiang Wei[2], and Yuyao Zhang[1,3(✉)]

[1] School of Information Science and Technology, ShanghaiTech University, Shanghai, China
zhangyy8@shanghaitech.edu.cn
[2] School of Biomedical Engineering, Shanghai Jiao Tong University, Shanghai, China
[3] Shanghai Engineering Research Center of Intelligent Vision and Imaging, ShanghaiTech University, Shanghai, China

Abstract. Longitudinal fetal brain atlas is a powerful tool for understanding and characterizing the complex process of fetus brain development. Existing fetus brain atlases are typically constructed by averaged brain images on discrete time points independently over time. Due to the differences in onto-genetic trends among samples at different time points, the resulting atlases suffer from temporal inconsistency, which may lead to estimating error of the brain developmental characteristic parameters along the timeline. To this end, we proposed a multi-stage deep-learning framework to tackle the time inconsistency issue as a 4D (3D brain volume + 1D age) image data denoising task. Using implicit neural representation, we construct a continuous and noise-free longitudinal fetus brain atlas as a function of the 4D spatial-temporal coordinate. Experimental results on two public fetal brain atlases (CRL and FBA-Chinese atlases) show that the proposed method can significantly improve the atlas temporal consistency while maintaining good fetus brain structure representation. In addition, the continuous longitudinal fetus brain atlases can also be extensively applied to generate finer 4D atlases in both spatial and temporal resolution.

Keywords: Longitudinal fetal brain atlases · Spatial-temporal consistency · Implicit neural representation · Image denoising

1 Introduction

The development of the fetal brain is a complex and dynamic process [16,20]. Abnormal development of the fetus brain may lead to long-term neurodevelopmental disorders and may even affect the quality of life in the perinatal and later childhood. Longitudinal fetal brain atlas is an important tool to boost the understanding of fetus brain development and provide a statistical standard of fetus

R. Licandro et al. (Eds.): PIPPI 2022, LNCS 13575, pp. 38–47, 2022.
https://doi.org/10.1007/978-3-031-17117-8_4

brain structure at different gestational ages. There have been few longitudinal fetus brain atlases [3,4,18,22], which constructed the averaging templates at discrete time points independently over time or simply added smoothing kernels on the age window. Due to the differences in onto-genetic trends among samples at different time points, the effect of noise along the developmental timeline is one of the most critical challenges for longitudinal atlas construction. Besides, limited by the image reconstruction quality of individual fetus brain, atlas quality may also suffer from reconstruction artifacts. Such issues will result in a certain precision error when quantifying the developmental characteristic parameters at each time point.

To address the temporal inconsistency issue in longitudinal atlas construction, Zhang et al. [24] proposed a 4D infant brain atlas construction method via introducing a temporal consistency term in the atlas sparse reconstruction. By incorporating the longitudinal constraint on a learning-based registration method, Chen et al. [2] proposed an age-conditional learning framework to construct 4D infant cerebellum atlas. Similarly, Zhao, F., et al. [25] proposed a similar temporal constraint on an unsupervised learning-based surface atlas construction. However, most of these mentioned works significantly depend on the specific data collection process. Specifically, these methods usually need a sequence of scans from the same subjects within the age range of interest, which are typically expensive and super challenging to acquire.

From another perspective, this problem could be modeled as a single four-dimensional (4D: 3D brain volume + 1D age) image data denoising problem that emphasizing to reduce noise along the timeline. This is because, the 3D image noise is largely reduced during the averaging template generation process, where the temporal consistency is normally not properly considered. The single image self-supervised denoising problem has been well-studied over the past several years. Ulyanov et al. [21] introduced deep image prior (DIP) to solve denoising problems by fitting the weights of an over-parameterized deep convolutional network to a single image, together with strong regularization by early stopping of the optimization. However, the hyper-parameters of early stopping are hard to tune, and the high-frequency content reduced by early stopping could be both noise and image details. In [11], Noise2Noise method proposes a statistically more meaningful manner to reduce only zero-mean image noise by learning the differences between two noisy observations of the same object. For avoiding using noisy image pairs as in [11], several single image denoising methods are designed to build specific blind-spot network structures to decrease image noise [7,10].

In this work, we propose a multi-stage learning framework to train and refine a continuous longitudinal fetus brain atlas that is continuous in both 3D coordinate and timeline. Overall, we iteratively refine the existing longitudinal fetus brain atlas with the temporal inconsistency problem via a 4D single image denoising task. Specifically, 1) As brain growth is highly continuous and follows certain trajectories, which could be fitted by a continuous function. We then use spatially encoded multi-layer perceptron network (MLP) [23] to implicitly represent the longitudinal atlas as a 4D (3D coordinate and time t) continuous image function; 2) However, the above method has the same issue as DIP [21].

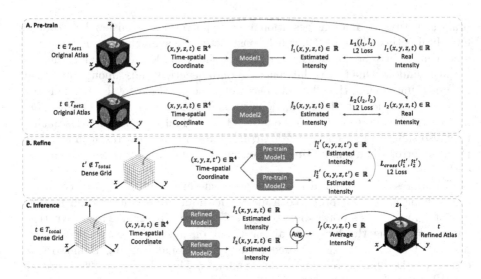

Fig. 1. An overview of the proposed continuous longitudinal fetus brain atlas construction framework.

The network has sufficient capacity to overfit image noise without early stopping. Thus, we divide the original longitudinally atlas into two different groups according to time points and approximate the 4D images in each of the two separated groups using two continuous functions. Since the two sets of atlases represent the same brain developing trajectory, the learned functions are theoretically equivalent. However, since the two networks overfit different image noise, two different functions are actually learned. By encouraging the atlases inferred by these two continuous functions at arbitrary new time point to be the same, we induce atlases with reduced noise along gestational age, i.e., better temporally-consistency; 3) By averaging the two final continuous functions, we construct the continuous longitudinal fetus brain atlas function. To the best of our knowledge, it is the first time to tackle the temporal inconsistency as a 4D image denoising problem and improve the consistency of existing atlases. Both qualitative and quantitative results demonstrate that comparing to the original atlas, the refined atlas achieves better time consistency while maintaining a good representation of fetus brain structure.

2   Method

An overview of our framework is depicted in Fig. 1, which is presented in three stages: a) Pre-train stage; b) Refine stage; c) Inference stage.

In this paper, we present a very simple yet effective method to train and refine a continuous 4D fetus brain atlas. Firstly, the original atlas set that includes N different time points $T_{total} = \{t_i\}_{i=1}^N$ are divided into two separated subgroups $T_{set1} = \{t_{2n-1}\}$ and $T_{set2} = \{t_{2n}\}$, where $n = 1, ..., N/2$ (as Fig. 1(A)). Then

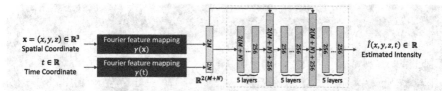

Fig. 2. Architecture of our model.

images in each of the group are approximated using a 4D continuous function $\hat{I}_1 = f_{\theta_1}(x, y, z, t), t \in T_{set1}$ and $\hat{I}_2 = f_{\theta_2}(x, y, z, t), t \in T_{set2}$. Secondly, series of novel time dependent brain images at time points $t' \notin T_{total}$ are generated as $\hat{I}_1^{t'} = f_{\theta_1}(x, y, z, t')$ and $\hat{I}_2^{t'} = f_{\theta_2}(x, y, z, t')$ (Fig. 1(B)). A denoising network is then trained by input image $\hat{I}_1^{t'}$ and labeled by image $\hat{I}_2^{t'}$ at the same time series of t'. The two stream refinement strategy satisfying the image denoising requirement as in [11] that paired pixels of paired images with independent noise and equivalent image content, and avoiding from using a second noisy image observation. Finally, by averaging the two continuous fetus brain function we learnt and refined, we construct the final temporally-continuous 4D fetus brain atlas function as $f_{\theta_{mean}}(x, y, z, t) = 1/2f_{\theta_1}(x, y, z, t) + 1/2f_{\theta_2}(x, y, z, t)$. By passing the series of time points as that from the original atlas series into the continuous atlas function $\hat{I}_f = f_{\theta_{mean}}(x, y, z, t), t \in T_{total}$, we reconstruct a longitudinally-consistent 4D series of fetus brain atlases (Fig. 1(C)).

2.1 Pre-train Stage

As demonstrated in Fig. 1(A), we first divide T_{total} into T_{set1} and T_{set2}. Then, we use two spatial encoded MLPs to approximate the 4D image per set as a continuous function. Specifically, we feed the voxel coordinate and time (x, y, z, t) into our model f_θ to compute the predicted voxel intensity $\hat{I}(x, y, z, t)$. We donate $\hat{I}$ as a explicit 4D image and $\hat{I}(x, y, z, t)$ as the intensity at location (x, y, z) and time t. We learn the parameters θ by minimizing the mean square error (MSE) loss function between the predicted voxel intensity and the real observed voxel intensity at current time point for a mini-batch of size, P. The loss function $\mathcal{L}$ is denoted as:

$$\mathcal{L}(\theta) = \frac{1}{|P|} \sum_{(x,y,z,t) \in P} ||I(x, y, z, t) - \hat{I}(x, y, z, t)||^2 \qquad (1)$$

Architecture of our Model. The architecture and training strategy is exactly same for Model1 and Model2 in Fig. 1(A). As illustrated in Fig. 2, our model consists of a encoding section and a MLP network, taking the 4D time-spatial coordinate input and outputting the corresponding intensity. For the encoding section, Mildenhall et al. [19] recently proposed Fourier feature mapping to overcome the spectral bias that the standard MLPs are biased towards learning lower frequency functions [15]. In our model, we perform Fourier feature mapping to

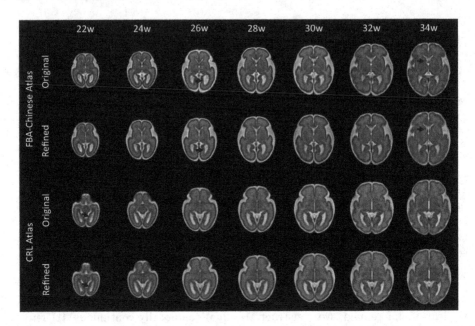

Fig. 3. Visual comparison overview of original and refined CRL and FBA-Chinese atlases. Note that although limited time points are shown, our framework provides temporally-continuous 4D atlases at arbitrary time points.

respectively map the 3D voxel coordinates and the time t to the higher dimensional space $\mathbb{R}^{2L}(2L > x, x = 1$ or 3) before passing them to the standard MLP network. Let $\gamma(\cdot)$ denotes Fourier feature mapping from the space $\mathbb{R}^x$ to $\mathbb{R}^{2L}$ and it is calculated by $\gamma(\mathbf{v}) = [\cos(2\pi\mathbf{Bv}), \sin(2\pi\mathbf{Bv})]^T$ where $\mathbf{v} \in \mathbb{R}^x$ and each element in $\mathbf{B} \in \mathbb{R}^{L \times x}$ is independently sampled from standard normal distribution $\mathcal{N}(0,1)$. For the MLP network, the network has eighteen fully-connected layers with two skip connections [5,6] that concatenate the input of the fully-connected network to the 6th and 12th layer's activation. Each fully-connected layer is followed by a batch normalization [8] layer and a ReLU [13] activation.

2.2   Refine Stage

The "refine" strategy is illustrated in Fig. 2(B). After the processing in Sect. 2.1, the two pre-trained models have already overfitted to the two subsets of the original longitudinally atlas with noise. Ideally, the two pre-trained models should approximate the same continuous function since the two 4D sub-images are sampled from the same 4D singe image (original longitudinal atlases) and represent the same brain developing trajectory. However, due to the models in the "pretrained" stage overfit to different image noise, the two networks are slightly different in fact. Inspired by Noise2Noise [11], we propose a "refine" stage to refine the pre-trained models and find the final continuous function, which could represent the continuous time-consistent 4D atlas.

We feed the image coordinate grid (x, y, z) with arbitrary new time points $t' \notin T_{total}$ to these two pre-trained models to generate two series of time dependent brain images $\hat{I}_1^{t'} = f_{\theta_1}(x, y, z, t')$ and $\hat{I}_2^{t'} = f_{\theta_2}(x, y, z, t')$. Because those two models tend to approximate the same brain developing trajectory, then we suppose the predicted voxel intensity in $\hat{I}_1^{t'}$ and $\hat{I}_2^{t'}$ should be identical. So we further iteratively update the parameters of the two pre-trained functions by minimizing the mean square error (MSE) loss function between the two predicted brain images at new time points. The formulation of loss function is similar to Eq. (1). Besides, we design an updated cut-off condition $\mathcal{L}_{total}$:

$$\mathcal{L}_{total} = \lambda \cdot \mathcal{L}_1 + \lambda \cdot \mathcal{L}_2 + \mathcal{L}_{cross} \qquad (2)$$

where $\mathcal{L}_1$ and $\mathcal{L}_2$ are the image fidelity loss between MLP functions and the corresponding real observations at T_{set1} and T_{set2}. While $\mathcal{L}_{cross}$ is the MSE loss between two predicted images $\hat{I}_1^{t'}$ and $\hat{I}_2^{t'}$ from two pre-trained models. λ is a hyper-parameter used to adjust the proportion of each loss. When $\mathcal{L}_{total}$ is minimal, the model we get is optimal.

2.3 Inference Stage

The sketch map of a longitudinally-consistent 4D fetus brain atlas reconstruction by the final refined model is shown in Fig. 2(C). Once the training is completed, we average the two continuous functions and construct the final continuous 4D fetus brain atlas function as $f_{\theta_{mean}}(x, y, z, t) = 1/2 f_{\theta_1}(x, y, z, t) + 1/2 f_{\theta_2}(x, y, z, t)$. Then given the age attribute t in T_{total}, we pass the voxel coordinate (x, y, z) with t into our final model to reconstruct a longitudinally-consistent 4D series of fetus brain atlases $\hat{I}_f = f_{\theta_{mean}}(x, y, z, t), t \in T_{total}$.

3 Experiments

3.1 Setup

Dataset. We evaluated the proposed framework on two existing public longitudinal fetus brain atlases: CRL atlas [3] and FBA-Chinese atlas [22]. CRL is constructed from MRI of 81 normal Caucasian fetuses scanned between 21 and 38 weeks of gestation. FBA-Chinese atlas is created from 115 normal Chinese fetal brains between 22 and 34 weeks of gestation.

Implementation Details. For CRL atlas, we set $T_{set1} = \{21, 23, 25, 27, 29, 31, 33, 35, 37, 38$ week$\}$, $T_{set2} = \{21, 22, 24, 26, 28, 30, 32, 34, 36, 38$ week$\}$ and arbitrary new time set$= \{t + 0.5\}_{t=21}^{37}$. For FBA-Chinese atlas, we set $T_{set1} = \{22, 24, 26, 28, 30, 32, 34, 35$ week$\}$, $T_{set2} = \{22, 23, 25, 27, 29, 31, 33, 35$ week$\}$ and arbitrary new time set $= \{t + 0.5\}_{t=22}^{34}$.

In "pre-train" stage, the Fourier feature mapping dimension $2L$ is set as 256 for 3D coordinate and 64 for time. Besides, our models are trained with a batch size of 25000 using an Adam [9] optimizer with $\beta = (0.9, 0.999)$. The learning rate starts from 10^{-4} and decays by factor 0.5 every 100 epochs. In "refine" stage, we set λ as 0.1 in cut-off condition $\mathcal{L}_{total}$.

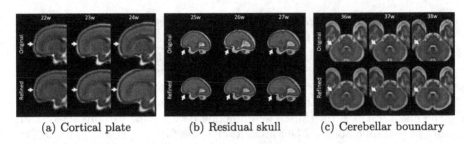

(a) Cortical plate   (b) Residual skull   (c) Cerebellar boundary

Fig. 4. Supplementary visual comparison in other views. (a) Comparison of cortical plate in CRL atlas. (b) Comparison of residual skull in FBA-Chinese atlas. (c) Comparison of cerebellar boundary in FBA-Chinese atlas.

3.2 Results

Visual Comparisons. Figure 3 provides typical axial examples of the CRL and FBA-Chinese atlases refined by proposed framework.

Generally, the proposed method illustrates clear denoising performance on both 3D image volume and 1D time line. For example, the image contrast in the basal ganglia regions is improved in the reconstructed brains. Besides, as arrow high-lighted, for the original **FBA-Chinese** atlas, the lateral ventricle of 26w atlas is significantly larger than that of 25w and 27w. The proposed model corrected this brain structure noise. Similarly, the vascular detail at 34w is refined. Figure 4 provides the results of other views and more detailed refinement in brain anatomical structures. Figure 4(a) shows that the cortical plate of original atlases has artifacts caused by motion, and the atlases obtained through our framework have a more consistent cortical plate. Figure 4(b) shows that our framework can effectively improve the inconsistency problem caused by incomplete skull stripping during atlas construction. For **CRL** atlas, the image contrast is improved at age 22w and ventricle structure is also refined. Besides, as can be seen from Fig. 4(c), the refined atlases obtain a more apparent cerebellar boundary.

Quantitative Comparision. We used three evaluation matrices: Entropy Focus Criterion (EFC), DICE coefficients and Time Consistency (TC) factor to evaluate our longitudinal fetus brain atlases. The results show that the atlases obtained by our method have better time consistency while ensuring good sharpness and representation. Detailed results are summarized in Table 1.

To evaluate the sharpness of our proposed atlases, we use Entropy Focus Criterion (EFC) [1,17] in MRQy [17]. The entropy focus criterion of the entire atlas image is defined as $EFC = \frac{1}{M} \sum_{m=1}^{M} (|S * \frac{1}{\sqrt{S}} \ln \frac{1}{\sqrt{S}}|)^{-1} * (-\sum_{s=1}^{S} \frac{x_s}{x_{max}} \ln \left[\frac{x_s}{x_{max}} \right])$ where S and M is the number of voxels and slices, m is the mth slice, and x_{max} is defined by $x_{max} = \sqrt{\sum_{s=1}^{S} x_s^2}$ with signal intensity x_s. The images that lack sharp distinctions between brain regions would have high entropy values [12]. Table 1 shows that the refined atlases have similar

Table 1. Quantitative comparison on CRL and FBA-Chinese atlases for sharpness(EFC), representation(DICE) and time consistency(TC). The best results are indicated in red.

			21	22	23	24	25	26	27	28	29	30	31	32	33	34	35	36	37	38
CRL	EFC	ori.	0.2018	0.2170	0.2218	0.2429	0.2722	0.2907	0.2888	0.3043	0.3166	0.3383	0.3405	0.3747	0.3773	0.3941	0.4095	0.4107	0.4107	0.4114
		ref.	0.2049	0.2181	0.2294	0.2435	0.2604	0.2932	0.2929	0.2899	0.2912	0.3241	0.3548	0.3771	0.3827	0.3989	0.4071	0.4140	0.4113	0.3646
	DICE	ori.	37.27	34.50	42.22	41.74	30.05	49.76	49.02	48.11	44.86	44.09	60.01	66.68	54.43	63.81	\	\	\	\
		ref.	41.66	37.34	44.99	43.39	40.39	52.05	51.76	49.17	46.69	47.51	63.55	71.00	57.03	73.52				
	TC	ori.	88.85	91.15	92.13	92.17	93.09	93.80	94.76	94.92	94.88	94.67	93.57	93.41	93.41	93.34	93.15	93.91	93.54	92.99
		ref.	89.31	91.92	92.94	92.75	93.32	94.31	94.79	95.17	94.98	94.67	93.82	93.66	93.73	93.69	93.40	94.20	93.82	93.57
FBA	EFC	ori.		0.2145	0.2158	0.2323	0.2652	0.2794	0.2910	0.3089	0.3179	0.3405	0.3472	0.3640	0.3619	0.3764	0.4027			
		ref.		0.2138	0.2153	0.2079	0.2312	0.2516	0.2685	0.2759	0.2927	0.3238	0.3459	0.3552	0.3627	0.3797	0.3761			
	DICE	ori.	\	35.34	42.85	40.67	31.59	52.29	48.57	47.35	44.49	46.86	62.27	67.84	53.67	64.62	\	\	\	\
		ref.		36.71	44.71	42.17	32.72	52.52	52.34	51.44	45.88	47.51	62.85	73.01	58.54	73.17				
	TC	ori.		91.27	92.23	92.09	91.26	91.31	92.74	92.96	91.21	92.44	90.79	90.96	87.16	86.59	83.25			
		ref.		91.47	93.08	91.99	92.78	93.50	94.40	94.12	92.55	92.95	92.01	94.26	90.86	91.51	85.18			

or even lower values than original atlases, indicating our refined atlases have a relatively comparable image quality with original atlases in terms of sharpness.

To evaluate the representativeness of the refined fetal brain atlas, we performed the atlas-based segmentation method [22] with Dice similarity coefficient to evaluate. We use the Fetal Tissue Annotation and Segmentation Dataset (FeTA) [14], which contains 50 manually segmented fetal brains across 20 to 33 weeks with 7 different regions-of-interest (ROI). Specifically, these subject images with ROI label were firstly registered to the refined atlas and the original atlas, respectively. Then DICE coefficients between different subjects in same atlas space are calculated and compared. A higher DICE value indicates a higher accuracy of the atlas for guiding brain anatomical normalization. Meanwhile, a higher DICE value can also indicate that the atlas has better consistency because the atlas with better consistency would lead to better registration result. Table 1 shows that the refined atlases have higher DICE than original atlases

In order to quantitatively analyze the temporal consistency for the atlas, we define the temporal consistency (TC) factor. Suppose $I_{atlas}^{LV}(t^m)(m = 1, \cdots, M)$ are the lateral ventricle maps for atlas image on the mth time point and $I_{atlas}^{LV}(t^m \to t^{m'})(m' = m \pm i, i = 1, 2)$ are the tissue label maps warped from $t^{m'}$ to t^m. Then the temporal consistency (TC) factor can be calculated as:

$$TC(t^m) = \frac{1}{|m'|} \sum_{m'} DICE\left(I_{atlas}^{LV}\left(t^{m'}\right), I_{atlas}^{LV}\left(t^m \to t^{m'}\right)\right) \qquad (3)$$

Thus, TCs of lateral ventricle reflect the temporal consistency of the tissue maps. Higher values indicate relatively better temporally consistent results. As shown in Table 1, our refined atlases correct the inconsistency time point and apparently improve the temporal consistency.

4 Conclusion

In this paper, we propose a multi-stage implicit neural representation framework to train and construct a longitudinally consistent 4D fetal brain atlas. Experimental results demonstrate that the denoised 4D fetal brain atlases achieve better time consistency and good brain structure representation both qualitatively and quantitatively. In addition, our framework can be extensively applied to other atlases and the continuous longitudinal fetus brain atlases we constructed can also be extensively applied to other tasks, such as constructing finer 4D atlases in both spatial or temporal resolution.

References

1. Atkinson, D., Hill, D.L., Stoyle, P.N., Summers, P.E., Keevil, S.F.: Automatic correction of motion artifacts in magnetic resonance images using an entropy focus criterion. IEEE Trans. Med. Imaging **16**(6), 903–910 (1997)
2. Chen, L., et al.: Construction of longitudinally consistent 4D infant cerebellum atlases based on deep learning. In: de Bruijne, M., et al. (eds.) MICCAI 2021. LNCS, vol. 12904, pp. 139–149. Springer, Cham (2021). https://doi.org/10.1007/978-3-030-87202-1_14
3. Gholipour, A., et al.: A normative spatiotemporal MRI atlas of the fetal brain for automatic segmentation and analysis of early brain growth. Sci. Rep. **7**(1), 1–13 (2017)
4. Habas, P.A., et al.: A spatiotemporal atlas of MR intensity, tissue probability and shape of the fetal brain with application to segmentation. Neuroimage **53**(2), 460–470 (2010)
5. He, K., Zhang, X., Ren, S., Sun, J.: Deep residual learning for image recognition. In: Proceedings of the IEEE Conference on Computer Vision and Pattern Recognition, pp. 770–778 (2016)
6. He, K., Zhang, X., Ren, S., Sun, J.: Identity mappings in deep residual networks. In: Leibe, B., Matas, J., Sebe, N., Welling, M. (eds.) ECCV 2016. LNCS, vol. 9908, pp. 630–645. Springer, Cham (2016). https://doi.org/10.1007/978-3-319-46493-0_38
7. Huang, T., Li, S., Jia, X., Lu, H., Liu, J.: Neighbor2neighbor: self-supervised denoising from single noisy images. In: Proceedings of the IEEE/CVF Conference on Computer Vision and Pattern Recognition, pp. 14781–14790 (2021)
8. Ioffe, S., Szegedy, C.: Batch normalization: accelerating deep network training by reducing internal covariate shift. In: International Conference on Machine Learning, pp. 448–456. PMLR (2015)
9. Kingma, D.P., Ba, J.: Adam: A method for stochastic optimization. arXiv preprint arXiv:1412.6980 (2014)
10. Krull, A., Buchholz, T.O., Jug, F.: Noise2void-learning denoising from single noisy images. In: Proceedings of the IEEE/CVF Conference on Computer Vision and Pattern Recognition, pp. 2129–2137 (2019)
11. Lehtinen, J., et al.: Noise2noise: learning image restoration without clean data. arXiv preprint arXiv:1803.04189 (2018)
12. Liu, X., Niethammer, M., Kwitt, R., Singh, N., McCormick, M., Aylward, S.: Low-rank atlas image analyses in the presence of pathologies. IEEE Trans. Med. Imaging **34**(12), 2583–2591 (2015)
13. Nair, V., Hinton, G.E.: Rectified linear units improve restricted Boltzmann machines. In: ICML (2010)
14. Payette, K., et al.: An automatic multi-tissue human fetal brain segmentation benchmark using the fetal tissue annotation dataset. Sci. Data **8**(1), 1–14 (2021)
15. Rahaman, N., et al.: On the spectral bias of neural networks. In: International Conference on Machine Learning, pp. 5301–5310. PMLR (2019)

16. Righini, A., et al.: Hippocampal infolding angle changes during brain development assessed by prenatal MR imaging. Am. J. Neuroradiol. **27**(10), 2093–2097 (2006)
17. Sadri, A.R., et al.: MRQY-an open-source tool for quality control of MR imaging data. Med. Phys. **47**(12), 6029–6038 (2020)
18. Serag, A., et al.: A multi-channel 4d probabilistic atlas of the developing brain: application to fetuses and neonates. Ann. BMVA **2012**(3), 1–14 (2012)
19. Tancik, M., et al.: Fourier features let networks learn high frequency functions in low dimensional domains. Adv. Neural. Inf. Process. Syst. **33**, 7537–7547 (2020)
20. Tilea, B., et al.: Cerebral biometry in fetal magnetic resonance imaging: new reference data. Ultrasound Obstet. Gynecol. **33**(2), 173–181 (2009)
21. Ulyanov, D., Vedaldi, A., Lempitsky, V.: Deep image prior. In: Proceedings of the IEEE Conference on Computer Vision and Pattern Recognition, pp. 9446–9454 (2018)
22. Wu, J., et al.: Age-specific structural fetal brain atlases construction and cortical development quantification for Chinese population. NeuroImage **241**, 118412 (2021) https://doi.org/10.1016/j.neuroimage.2021.118412, https://www.sciencedirect.com/science/article/pii/S105381192100687X
23. Wu, Q., et al.: IREM: high-resolution magnetic resonance image reconstruction via implicit neural representation. In: de Bruijne, M., et al. (eds.) MICCAI 2021. LNCS, vol. 12906, pp. 65–74. Springer, Cham (2021). https://doi.org/10.1007/978-3-030-87231-1_7
24. Zhang, Y., et al.: Consistent spatial-temporal longitudinal atlas construction for developing infant brains. IEEE Trans. Med. Imaging **35**(12), 2568–2577 (2016)
25. Zhao, F., Wu, Z., Wang, L., Lin, W., Xia, S., Li, G.: Learning 4D infant cortical surface atlas with unsupervised spherical networks. In: de Bruijne, M., et al. (eds.) MICCAI 2021. LNCS, vol. 12902, pp. 262–272. Springer, Cham (2021). https://doi.org/10.1007/978-3-030-87196-3_25

Automated Segmentation of Cervical Anatomy to Interrogate Preterm Birth

Alicia B. Dagle[1] , Yucheng Liu[2] , David Crosby[3] , Helen Feltovich[4],
Michael House[5] , Qi Yan[6] , Kristin M. Myers[1] ,
and Sachin Jambawalikar[2](✉)

[1] Department of Mechanical Engineering, Columbia University,
New York, NY 10027, USA
abd2150@cumc.columbia.edu
[2] Department of Radiology, Columbia University Irving Medical Center,
New York, NY 10032, USA
sj2532@cumc.columbia.edu
[3] Department of Obstetrics and Gynecology, National Maternity Hospital
and University College, Dublin, Leinster D02 YH21, Ireland
[4] Maternal Fetal Medicine, Intermountain Healthcare, Provo, UT 84604, USA
[5] Department of Obstetrics and Gynecology, Tufts Medical Center,
Boston, MA 02111, USA
[6] Department of Obstetrics and Gynecology, Columbia University Irving Medical
Center, New York, NY 10032, USA

Abstract. A safe, full-term pregnancy is vital to the health and well-being of every child, yet it is far from guaranteed. Preterm birth (PTB) is the leading cause of perinatal death and remains a major global health concern. Due to limited pregnancy-related research, clinicians cannot fully explain what triggers healthy, gestationally-appropriate labor, let alone risky premature labor. This lack of fundamental understanding hinders the ability to predict PTB on an individual patient level. This work focuses on the cervix, a complex biomechanical barrier in pregnancy. Sonographic measurement of cervical length with transvaginal ultrasound (TVUS) is a common clinical test to assess the risk of subsequent PTB. Accurate sonographic cervix segmentation followed by multi-dimensional cervical geometric feature extraction is hypothesized to have a higher PTB predictive capability compared to sonographic cervical length alone. The computational tool developed in this study segments the entire cross-sectional area of the cervix tissue from 2D transvaginal ultrasounds, enabling the creation of a generalizable, cervical-features-based prediction model of PTB risk. Manual segmentation methods are time-consuming, not scale-able, and can vary between clinicians and sonographers. Thus, an automatic deep learning based multi-class residual UNet architecture segmentation method is employed. The model is trained on data from the Cervical Length Education and Review (CLEAR) program, which includes second and third trimester TVUS images from multiple sites and ultrasound systems across the United States. This work demonstrates standard-of-care TVUS may be used to accurately segment cervical geometry, enabling the study of cervical variations across pregnancies with broader implications in understanding and ultimately preventing PTB.

Keywords: preterm birth · segmentation · cervix

1 Introduction

Preterm birth (PTB), defined as delivery before 37 weeks of gestation, is the leading cause of perinatal death [4] and a major contributor to long-term disabilities [6], where lower gestational age at birth corresponds to longer hospital stays, increased risk of long-term symptoms, and increased medical costs [9]. With persistently high global rates of PTB and 15 million premature births estimated yearly, PTB remains a major public health problem with high emotional and financial burden [5,10]. Despite significant advances in prenatal and perinatal care, 80% of PTBs result from spontaneous preterm birth (sPTB), defined as premature labor or rupture of fetal membranes leading to preterm delivery. Prediction of sPTB is difficult, especially among patients without prior history of sPTB [16], hindering the development of early interventions and preventative treatments.

Multiple studies have explored ultrasound measurements for the prediction of sPTB, including cervical length (CL), anterior uterocervical angle (AUCA), lower uterine segment (LUS) thickness, and degree of funneling [27]. However, only CL has demonstrated clinical significance as a stand-alone, reproducible indicator of sPTB [13]. Accordingly, the clinical gold standard to evaluate sPTB risk for a specific pregnancy is sonographic assessment of CL, measured from 2D, transvaginal ultrasound (TVUS) images [21]. Measurements taken during the second and third trimester, require adherence to stringent guidelines such as the Cervical Length Education and Review (CLEAR) criteria to ensure accuracy [12]. While a short cervix is an important predictor of sPTB, with lower CL correlating with higher incidence of sPTB [12], the positive predictive value (PPV) of CL alone is limited [21], ranging from 26–52% for women with no history of preterm birth [20]. Thus, improved sPTB prediction methods are needed.

The cervix is a complex, 3D biomechanical [14] and immunological [19] barrier that protects the growing fetus and remodels to facilitate birth. The structural failure of the cervix, as seen in premature cervical remodeling and shortening, is a common feature of sPTB [23]. 3D biomechanical models suggest the overall shape, volume, and intrinsic material properties determine cervical mechanical performance [7,24]. Additionally, the alignment of the cervix with the uterus determines how the load of the growing fetus is directed [24]. Therefore, CL is an incomplete measure of cervical barrier and biomechanical function.

Convolutional neural networks (CNNs) have recently gained popularity in biomedical image segmentation [18]. While traditional single-class UNet, and DeepLabV3 architectures have been explored for cervical segmentation [25], multi-class networks and other more-complex architectures have not yet been applied. A single-class UNet successfully segmented curves approximating cervical shape, to then extract CL and anterior cervical angle, and feed these measurements and original images into PTB prediction models [26]. However, no deep learning framework has segmented the anterior and posterior cervical tissue and cervical canal space differentially. The ability to distinguish these tissue regions will ultimately allow algorithms to extract more biomechanically relevant features including LUS thickness, anterior/posterior cervical diameter, and closed cervical area as well as previously recorded CL and AUCA measurements.

In this work, patient variations in cervical geometry during the second and third trimesters of pregnancy are explored. A novel tool is introduced to segment the entire 2D cervical region from TVUS images of pregnant patients into multiple anatomical classes including: anterior cervical tissue, posterior cervical tissue, and cervical canal space. These predictions are performed on a pixel-by-pixel basis where the introduction of a multi-class model helps identify boundaries between neighboring structures. Traditionally, labeling ultrasounds with this level of detail is highly time-consuming, labor-intensive, and subject to variation between experts with differing clinical experience. An automated tool to label cervical anatomy will enable extraction of more detailed cervical geometry markers, further elucidating new etiologies of PTB. Ultimately, these 2D cervical shape mappings and extracted cervical features may enable the creation of a PTB prediction model which takes high-fidelity cervical feature inputs and outputs clinical risk of PTB.

2 Methods

2.1 Dataset

Images. The Perinatal Quality Foundation (PQF), which hosts the CLEAR training program [1], supplied the TVUS images which were used to train our deep learning segmentation networks. This diverse dataset consists of 250 TVUS images submitted for review to the CLEAR program, collected between 16–32 weeks gestation from different centers, ultrasound machines, and clinicians across the United States. Images were graded based upon their adherence to 9 CLEAR criteria, defined in Fig. 1, where a minimum score of 7 is required to pass. Of the 250 images in our dataset, 175 received a perfect score (grade 9), 50 received a passing score (grade 8), and 25 received a failing score (grade 6). An example image from each grading class is shown in Fig. 1. Ideally, all TVUS scans would merit a perfect score, but a small subset of real-world data is expected to fail CLEAR criteria due to human error, even after appropriate training. To further improve the model's ability to generalize, a small subset of grade 6 images were included in the dataset, as they still meet over half of the CLEAR criteria but fail to pass certification. Since the provided TVUS images were anonymized, no pregnancy outcome information is available and it is assumed that patients do not have repeat images in the dataset. Further inspection of the images, as depicted in Fig 2, reveals that short cervices (CL < 2.5 cm) and cervical funneling are present in roughly 15 % and 12% of images, respectively.

CLEAR Criteria:

1. exam is transvaginal
2. maternal bladder is empty
3. field of view is optimized
4. anterior cervical width = posterior cervical width
5. internal os is well seen
6. external os is well seen
7. endocervical canal is visible in its entirety
8. calipers are correctly placed
9. shortest, best of 3 measurements is reported

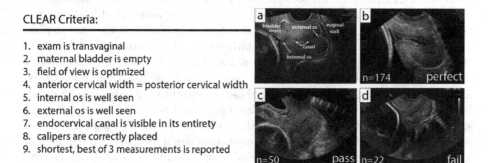

Fig. 1. a) A CLEAR certified image with demarcations of anatomical landmarks, b) Perfect grade 9/9 image satisfies all CLEAR criteria, c) Passing grade 8/9 image does not satisfy criteria #2, d) Failing grade 6/9 image does not satisfy criteria #3, 4, 9.

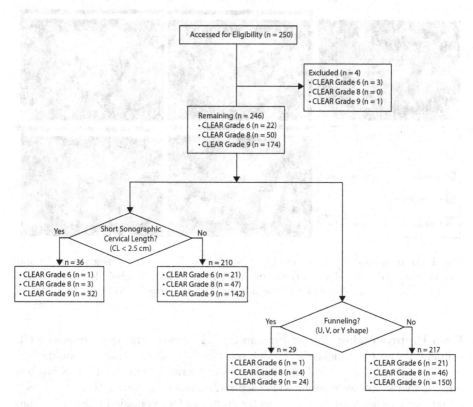

Fig. 2. Cohort flow chart illustrating quantity of excluded data. Population is further categorized based upon short cervical length (<2.5 cm) and the presence of cervical funneling (inclusive of grade 6, 8 and 9 images).

Labels. A CLEAR certified sonographer and 2 clinicians provided annotations using the segmentation software Labelbox [2]. During review and label generation, expert maskers were permitted to skip an image if the quality was too poor to distinguish the anatomic regions of interest (exclusion criteria in Fig. 2). Of the 250 original images, 4 images were excluded from the dataset during expert review leaving 174, 50, and 22 images in the grade 9, 8 and 6 groups, respectively. Experts were tasked with segmenting these images into 5 regions (background, bladder, anterior cervix + LUS, posterior cervix, and cervical canal + potential space) as shown in the segmentation label anatomy key of Fig. 3. Fleiss' kappa coefficient was calculated to determine agreement among experts. Across all 246 images in the labeled dataset, the Fleiss' kappa coefficient was 0.87, showing high agreement between experts. A majority choice voting system (illustrated in Fig. 3) was then used to generate ground truth (GT) labels for training, based on these 3 expert labels; if at least 2 experts labeled a pixel with a given class, then that pixel was set to true for that given class in the GT label.

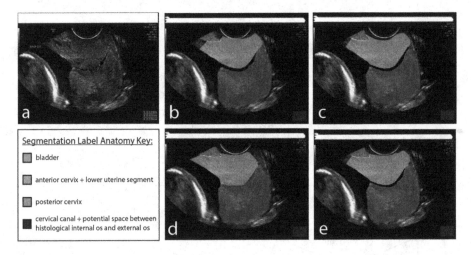

Fig. 3. An unlabeled TVUS image (a) is labeled by 3 experts: 1 sonographer (b) and 2 clinicians (c, d) according to the segmentation key. The GT label, determined by a majority voting method applied to the 3 expert masks is displayed (e).

Data Preprocessing. The cv2 inpainting [22] package was used to remove CL calipers placed by clinicians. The dataset was divided into training, validation, and test sets using a 70:20:10 split. Each set had a random distribution of images, but CLEAR scores were balanced in each set. Data augmentation techniques such as 180° rotations, random zoom, center crop, random Gaussian noise, Gaussian blur, and random contrast adjustments were applied only to the training set.

2.2   Model Architecture

For all model architectures, image/mask pairs are resized to 256×256 pixels, and the mask is one-hot encoded before training. The images are converted to grayscale and pixel values are normalized between 0 and 1, providing a 1-channel input to the network. The model computes a 5-channel output corresponding to background and the 4 classes depicted in Fig. 3. All model architectures are implemented using the MONAI library [3]. A multi-class residual UNet 2D CNN architecture [11] is trained with 5 convolutional layers (corresponding to 16, 32, 64, 128, and 256 channels), and a stride length of 2. Multi-class 2D Attention UNet [17], SegResNet [15], and transformer UNet (UNETR) [8] are also explored as alternative network architectures, where attention UNet is trained on the same 5 convolutional layers, and default values are used for SegResNet and UNETR implementations.

Model training monitors Dice loss and Dice metric. An average Dice metric value is calculated for each epoch by averaging class-specific dice metric across every class except background. During training, the model is allowed to run for 50 epochs, and early stopping monitors the validation loss with a patience of 5 epochs, but saves the model checkpoint with the best average Dice metric on the validation set during training. Predictions are generated by feeding inputs through the trained model, applying softmax activation along the class dimension and reporting the argmax value along the class dimension to determine the predicted class of each pixel in an image.

Hyperparameter Optimization. Both Adam and SGD optimizers were considered with learning rates ranging from 0.001 to 0.01 and 0.001 to 0.1, respectively. Dropout was varied between 0 and 0.6 in increments of 0.2. When considering the multi-class UNet, a traditional UNet and a residual UNet architecture were employed, by varying the number of residual units from 0 and 4, in increments of 2.

Hardware and Software. All models were executed on a single Tesla V100-32GB GPU. Model training was performed in Python 3.9, using PyTorch and MONAI [3] packages. Code for training and evaluating model performance is available at https://github.com/cumcrad/MulticlassSegmentationTVUS.

3   Results

For the multi-class residual U-Net architecture, model performance was optimized with the following hyper-parameters: Adam (learning rate = 0.001) or SGD (learning rate = 0.1) optimizer, dropout of 0.2, and 4 residual units. The difference in best model performance between Adam and SGD optimizers was

Table 1. Average Dice metric (DM), Hausdorff distance (HD), Jaccard index (JI) and associated standard deviations across all test image are tabulated. Attention UNet and SegResNet architectures performed comparably to the residual UNet.

Metric	Model Type			
	Residual UNet	Attention UNet	SegResNet	Transformer UNet
DM	0.80 ± 0.08	0.80 ± 0.08	0.80 ± 0.07	0.62 ± 0.06
HD	19.73 ± 10.23	24.39 ± 13.055	24.67 ± 12.89	73.49 ± 16.88
JI	0.72 ± 0.09	0.71 ± 0.09	0.72 ± 0.075	0.492 ± 0.065

negligible. Subsequent hyperparameter search, using only Adam optimizer, on the attention U-Net architecture found the same values: a learning rate of 0.001, and dropout of 0.2. Given this overlap in optimal hyperparameters, these values were adopted for all 4 model architectures, with results shown in Table 1.

Comparisons of Dice metric, Hausdorff distance, and Jaccard index indicate attention UNet and SegResNet performed comparably to the residual UNet. Further inspection of test images indicate attention UNet and SegResNet architectures had higher instances of image artifacts such as disconnected segmentation classes among the predicted images. One-way paired ANOVA followed by a paired multiple comparison T-test with Bonferroni corrections were used to compare the performance of each model in terms of Dice metric, Hausdorff distance, and Jaccard index. These statistical tests confirmed that only the transformer UNet performance differed with statistical significance (adjusted $p < 0.05$) against other models in terms of Dice metric, Hausdorff distance, and Jaccard index. This poor transformer UNet performance is likely attributed to small dataset size. Attention UNet and transformer UNet performance may improve given more training examples because of their ability to highlight important features [17], or capture long-range dependencies, global context and spatial information [8] respectively. Given its superior performance for these data and relatively small computational cost, the multi-class residual UNet model was used for the remainder of this work.

As shown in Fig. 4d, the multi-class residual 2D UNet model trained for 5.5 h and was saved after 16 epochs. Class-specific values of Dice metric, Hausdorff distance, and Jaccard index were calculated on the images in the test set and reported in Table 2. To ensure the inclusion of grade 6 images did not negatively affect model performance, the multi-class residual UNet architecture (4 residual units, Adam optimizer, learning rate = 0.001, dropout = 0.2) was retrained using only grade 8 and 9 images in the training and validation set. The inclusion or exclusion of the grade 6 images had no noticeable effect on the test performance, when evaluated both with and without the grade 6 images in the test set.

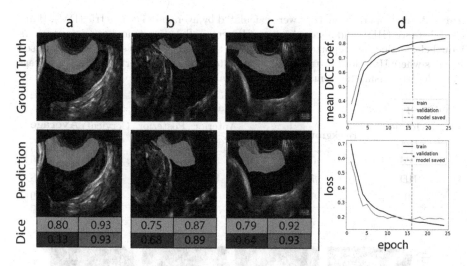

Fig. 4. Ground truth and prediction labels in the validation set demonstrate good model performance for variations in cervical geometry including: a) long curved cervix, b) short squat cervix, and c) median width/length cervix. Image specific dice scores are reported according to class color. d) Training and validation mean dice score (top) and loss (bottom) are plotted against the number of epochs to visualize model training.

Table 2. Dice metric (DM), Hausdorff distance (HD), and Jaccard index (JI) are tabulated for the best performing mutli-class residual UNet architecture. Class-specific average metrics and standard deviations are calculated across all images in test set.

Metric	Class				
	Background	Bladder	Anterior Cervix	Posterior Cervix	Cervical Canal
DM	0.98 ± 0.02	0.68 ± 0.23	0.91 ± 0.04	0.90 ± 0.07	0.55 ± 0.24
HD	17.71 ± 10.88	14.76 ± 12.24	16.12 ± 7.87	18.69 ± 14.04	31.38 ± 12.93
JI	0.95 ± 0.04	0.55 ± 0.23	0.84 ± 0.06	0.83 ± 0.10	0.41 ± 0.23

As a benchmark for inter-operator variability, agreement metrics (Dice metric, Hausdorff distance and Jaccard index) were calculated between the majority ground truth label and each expert label on the test set. These three metrics were then averaged across all experts to derive inter-operator values, reported in Table 3. For the test set, the inter-operator Dice score, averaged across all classes except background is 0.82, with class specific Dice scores of 0.94 for both anterior and posterior cervix classes. When evaluated on the test set, the best-performing multi-class residual UNet model achieved a high Dice score of 0.80 averaged across every class except the background, with class-specific Dice scores of 0.91 and 0.90 for the anterior and posterior cervix class, respectively. Therefore, the model performs only slightly below the agreement of clinical experts.

Table 3. Inter-operator metrics were calculated by averaging Dice metric (DM), Hausdorff distance (HD), and Jaccard index (JI) across all 3 experts and test images. Individual class values are reported, in addition to the average across segmentation classes. In cases where Hausdorff distance was an infinite value for 1 expert, * indicates average was calculated using the remaining 2 expert values.

Inter-operator Metric	Class					Average
	Background	Bladder	Anterior Cervix	Posterior Cervix	Cervical Canal	
DM	0.98	0.82	0.94	0.94	0.59	0.85
HD	17.47	*7.24	13.47	13.61	*57.57	*23.18
JI	0.97	0.74	0.88	0.89	0.47	0.79

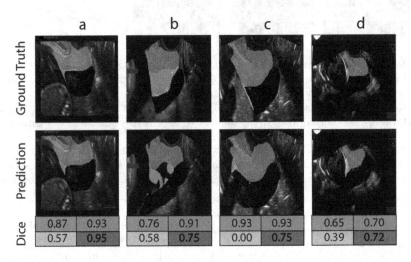

Fig. 5. Model performance limitations are depicted for validation images where certain artifacts limit reliability: a) The presence of a full bladder, b) funneling, c) a low-laying placenta, and d) an extremely zoomed-out field of view hinder model performance.

Limitations. Despite high performance on the test set, the bladder boundary is inaccurately predicted in images with a full bladder (Fig. 5a) likely because these images fail to meet CLEAR criteria (Fig. 1). In addition, the bladder is one of the smallest features in the TVUS images. Therefore, the bladder class occupies a small portion of labeled pixels in the dataset, which may cause the bladder segmentation results to be poor as compared to other classes. In the event of extreme funneling (Fig. 5b), visualized as a U, V, or Y-shaped internal os region, the model may struggle to find the histological internal os of the cervix. Again, this is likely attributed to there being fewer examples of funneled cervices compared to closed cervices in the data set. The low representation of funneling, associated with higher risk pregnancies, may unintentionally encourage the model to learn that the cervical canal + potential space class has fewer pixels than the other classes, which may lead to under-prediction of funnel shapes. If the placenta is located near the internal os (Fig. 5c), the placenta tissue is often mistaken for posterior cervix tissue, likely due to its similar sonographic brightness and texture. Finally, if the image violates CLEAR criteria because the cervix area is small relative to the field of view (Fig. 5d), the cervical area is sometimes over-predicted or misplaced.

In the future, including more images of short cervices, funneled cervices, and low-lying placentas may improve the model's ability to generalize. While more TVUS scans with a full bladder may help model generalizability, this goes against CLEAR criteria and therefore may not be recommended. As more images are introduced to the dataset, further hyperparameter search is needed to optimizer parameters for all 4 models individually. In particular, the SegResNet and UNETR architectures were not subject to a comprehensive hyperparameter search and should be explored in more detail.

4   Conclusion

This work develops an automated, multi-class segmentation network to label the cervical tissue in its entirety. Compared to previous work [25] segmenting only 1 class approximating the cervix, this multi-class model achieves a similar Dice score of 0.9 for both anterior and posterior cervix classes. Additionally, this model provides more information about the biomechanical loading angle between the uterus and the cervix by including a portion of the LUS in the label scheme.

Future work is indicated to improve the predictions for the bladder and cervical canal classes, which are used primarily as markers to better identify the cervix and anterior LUS tissue in this multi-class framework. The bladder, while holding little meaning as a stand-alone feature, may also act as a helpful landmark to aid a cervical feature extraction model. Although bladder predictions were less reliable than cervix predictions, the inclusion of the bladder class in this model is believed to improve the overall performance by providing a reliable, highly-echogenic landmark with an anatomically prescribed location near the anterior/superior boundary of the cervix. Similarly, the cervical canal class may also be used to examine the shape and size of a funnel or cervical mucus plug, if present in the TVUS image.

This novel tool has broad applications in studying the impact of cervical geometry variations on pregnancy outcomes, with a particular focus on sPTB. For this application, the model should be evaluated and fine-tuned on a larger dataset including preterm/term birth outcomes linked to TVUS images. The labeled outputs of this network can also be used to extract geometric features such as CL, cervical diameter, AUCA, LUS thickness, and closed cervical area. These input features can later be fed to prediction models for more robust, individualized patient predictions of sPTB risk. Furthermore, these labeled classes may be leveraged during real-time ultrasound scanning to determine if an image meets minimum requirements such as CLEAR criteria. This feedback may improve the reproducibility of TVUS scans and associated predictive capability of CL screening for sPTB.

This segmentation tool holds great promise in elucidating the pathways of sPTB, but more research is needed to fine-tune this model and ensure generalizability. Future work will include geometric feature extraction and validation against clinically reported values. Ultimately, this work may lead to an engineered PTB diagnostic method interrogating the biomechanical process of sPTB and a clinical workflow fitting practically into modern obstetrics care.

Acknowledgements. This study was supported in part by National Science Foundation Graduate Research Fellowship Grant DGE-2036197 to Alicia B. Dagle, and by Columbia University SEAS Interdisciplinary Research Seed (SIRS) Funding. TVUS images were provided by the Perinatal Quality Foundation and were collected as part of the CLEAR training program. We sincerely thank Keri Johnson of Intermountain Health for her expertise in providing anatomical segmentations of TVUS images. We would also like to thank Chai-Ling Nhan-Chang, MD of Columbia University for her feedback and insight during the ideation of the segmentation labels for this project.

References

1. Cervical Length Education and Review Program. https://clear.perinatalquality. org
2. Labelbox: https://labelbox.com/
3. MONAI - Home. https://monai.io/
4. Preterm birth. https://www.who.int/news-room/fact-sheets/detail/preterm-birth
5. Blencowe, H., et al.: National, regional, and worldwide estimates of preterm birth rates in the year 2010 with time trends since 1990 for selected countries: a systematic analysis and implications. Lancet **379**(9832), 2162–2172 (2012). https://doi. org/10.1016/S0140-6736(12)60820-4
6. Callaghan, W.M., MacDorman, M.F., Rasmussen, S.A., Qin, C., Lackritz, E.M.: The contribution of preterm birth to infant mortality rates in the united states. Pediatrics **118**(4), 1566–1573 (2006). https://doi.org/10.1542/peds.2006-0860
7. Fernandez, M., et al.: Investigating the mechanical function of the cervix during pregnancy using finite element models derived from high-resolution 3D MRI. Comput. Methods Biomech. Biomed. Engin. **19**(4), 404–417 (2016). https://doi.org/10. 1080/10255842.2015.1033163
8. Hatamizadeh, A., et al.: UNETR: Transformers for 3D Medical Image Segmentation, October 2021. https://doi.org/10.48550/arXiv.2103.10504, arXiv:2103.10504 [cs, eess]
9. Institute of Medicine (US) Committee on Understanding Premature Birth and Assuring Healthy Outcomes: Preterm Birth: Causes, Consequences, and Prevention. The National Academies Collection: Reports funded by National Institutes of Health, National Academies Press (US), Washington (DC) (2007)
10. Kassabian, S., Fewer, S., Yamey, G., Brindis, C.D.: Building a global policy agenda to prioritize preterm birth: a qualitative analysis on factors shaping global health policymaking. Gates Open Res. **4**, 65 (2020). https://doi.org/10.12688/ gatesopenres.13098.1

11. Kerfoot, E., Clough, J., Oksuz, I., Lee, J., King, A.P., Schnabel, J.A.: Left-ventricle quantification using residual U-Net. In: Pop, M., et al. (eds.) STACOM 2018. LNCS, vol. 11395, pp. 371–380. Springer, Cham (2019). https://doi.org/10.1007/978-3-030-12029-0_40

12. McIntosh, J., Feltovich, H., Berghella, V., Manuck, T.: The role of routine cervical length screening in selected high- and low-risk women for preterm birth prevention. Am. J. Obstet. Gynecol. **215**(3), B2–B7 (2016). https://doi.org/10.1016/j.ajog.2016.04.027

13. Mella, M.T., Berghella, V.: Prediction of preterm birth: cervical sonography. Semin. Perinatol. **33**(5), 317–324 (2009). https://doi.org/10.1053/j.semperi.2009.06.007

14. Myers, K.M., et al.: The mechanical role of the cervix in pregnancy. J. Biomech. **48**(9), 1511–1523 (2015). https://doi.org/10.1016/j.jbiomech.2015.02.065

15. Myronenko, A.: 3D MRI brain tumor segmentation using autoencoder regularization. arXiv:1810.11654 [cs, q-bio], November 2018

16. Norwitz, E.: UpToDate. UpToDate, Waltham, MA (2015). http://www.uptodate.com/contents/prevention-of-spontaneous-preterm-birth, section: Prevention of spontaneous preterm birth

17. Oktay, O., et al.: Attention U-Net: Learning Where to Look for the Pancreas, May 2018. arXiv:1804.03999 [cs]

18. Ronneberger, O., Fischer, P., Brox, T.: U-net: convolutional networks for biomedical image segmentation. In: Navab, N., Hornegger, J., Wells, W.M., Frangi, A.F. (eds.) MICCAI 2015. LNCS, vol. 9351, pp. 234–241. Springer, Cham (2015). https://doi.org/10.1007/978-3-319-24574-4_28

19. Simhan, H.N., Krohn, M.A.: First-trimester cervical inflammatory milieu and subsequent early preterm birth. Am. J. Obstet. Gynecol. **200**(4), 377.e1-377.e4 (2009). https://doi.org/10.1016/j.ajog.2008.10.038

20. Son, M., Miller, E.S.: Predicting preterm birth: cervical length and fetal fibronectin. Sem. Perinatol. **41**(8), 445–451 (2017). https://doi.org/10.1053/j.semperi.2017.08.002, https://www.sciencedirect.com/science/article/pii/S0146000517300903

21. Spong, C.Y.: Prediction and prevention of recurrent spontaneous preterm birth. Obstet. Gynecol. **110**(2 Part 1), 405–415 (2007). https://doi.org/10.1097/01.AOG.0000275287.08520.4a

22. Telea, A.: An image inpainting technique based on the fast marching method. J. Graph. Tools **9**(1), 23–34 (2004). https://doi.org/10.1080/10867651.2004.10487596

23. Vink, J., Feltovich, H.: Cervical etiology of spontaneous preterm birth. Semin. Fetal Neonatal. Med. **21**(2), 106–112 (2016). https://doi.org/10.1016/j.siny.2015.12.009

24. Westervelt, A.R., et al.: A parameterized ultrasound-based finite element analysis of the mechanical environment of pregnancy. J. Biomech. Eng. **139**(5), 051004 (2017). https://doi.org/10.1115/1.4036259

25. Włodarczyk, T., et al.: Spontaneous preterm birth prediction using convolutional neural networks. In: Hu, Y., et al. (eds.) ASMUS/PIPPI -2020. LNCS, vol. 12437, pp. 274–283. Springer, Cham (2020). https://doi.org/10.1007/978-3-030-60334-2_27

26. Włodarczyk, T., et al.: Machine learning methods for preterm birth prediction: a review. Electronics **10**(5), 586 (2021). https://doi.org/10.3390/electronics10050586

27. Yost, N.P.,et al.: For the national institute of child health and human development, MFMUN: second-trimester cervical sonography: features other than cervical length to predict spontaneous preterm birth. Obstet. Gynecol. **103**(3), 457–462 (2004). https://doi.org/10.1097/01.AOG.0000113618.24824.fb

Deep Learning Framework for Real-Time Fetal Brain Segmentation in MRI

Razieh Faghihpirayesh[1,2]($\boxtimes$), Davood Karimi[2], Deniz Erdoğmuş[1], and Ali Gholipour[2]

[1] Electrical and Computer Engineering Department, Northeastern University, Boston, USA
raziehfaghih@ece.neu.edu

[2] Radiology Department, Boston Children's Hospital; and Harvard Medical School, Boston, MA 02115, USA

Abstract. Fetal brain segmentation is an important first step for slice-level motion correction and slice-to-volume reconstruction in fetal MRI. Fast and accurate segmentation of the fetal brain on fetal MRI is required to achieve real-time fetal head pose estimation and motion tracking for slice re-acquisition and steering. To address this critical unmet need, in this work we analyzed the speed-accuracy performance of a variety of deep neural network models, and devised a symbolically small convolutional neural network that combines spatial details at high resolution with context features extracted at lower resolutions. We used multiple branches with skip connections to maintain high accuracy while devising a parallel combination of convolution and pooling operations as an input downsampling module to further reduce inference time. We trained our model as well as eight alternative, state-of-the-art networks with manually-labeled fetal brain MRI slices and tested on two sets of normal and challenging test cases. Experimental results show that our network achieved the highest accuracy and lowest inference time among all of the compared state-of-the-art real-time segmentation methods. We achieved average Dice scores of 97.99% and 84.04% on the normal and challenging test sets, respectively, with an inference time of 3.36 milliseconds per image on an NVIDIA GeForce RTX 2080 Ti. Code, data, and the trained models are available at this repo.

Keywords: Fetal MRI · Fetal brain · Real-time segmentation

1 Introduction

Fetal MRI is an important tool for diagnosis of abnormalities of the fetal brain during pregnancy due to its superior soft tissue contrast compared to ultrasound. However, MRI is very susceptible to motion and fetuses can move significantly during MRI scans. To mitigate this problem, fast MRI acquisition techniques are used to obtain stacks of 2D slices. Super-resolution techniques can then reconstruct 3D images from these 2D slices [3,4,6,8,12,26]. Segmentation of the brain

R. Licandro et al. (Eds.): PIPPI 2022, LNCS 13575, pp. 60–70, 2022.
https://doi.org/10.1007/978-3-031-17117-8_6

in slices can improve inter-slice motion correction and super-resolution recon-struction [27]. Real-time fetal brain segmentation on slices is needed to enable real-time fetal head pose estimation, motion tracking, and slice navigation [25].

While several studies have addressed 3D fetal brain segmentation on stack-of-slices or reconstructed fetal MRI scans [1,3,10,23], only a few studies have addressed the more challenging task of segmenting the fetal brain on every slice. Keraudren et al. [9] developed a method based on support vector machines and random forests. More recent works have almost exclusively been based on deep learning (DL), and in particular convolutional neural networks (CNNs). These methods are more suitable for real-time applications because they can harness the parallel computation capabilities of Graphical Processing Units (GPUs) [21]. Salehi et al. [24] used a DL method based on the U-Net architecture [22]. Wang et al. [28] computed aleatoric uncertainty and used test time augmentation to improve the accuracy of fetal brain segmentation on 2D slices. While these works focused on improving segmentation accuracy, none of them addressed the accuracy-speed trade-off. To address this gap, in this paper we focused on improving inference speed as well as accuracy.

Many applications demand real-time image processing. This demand has given rise to a growing body of real-time DL-based methods [17]. The majority of these works have aimed at reducing the computation time by devising lighter or special-ized network architectures. A typical example of architectural innovations is the depthwise-separable convolution, which breaks down a 3D convolution operation into a succession of 2D and 1D convolutions [7]. Another approach to reducing the computational cost is channel shuffling as used in ShuffleNets [16,30]. Gamal et al. [5] proposed ShuffleSeg based on ShuffleNet by using ShuffleNet with grouped convolutions, channel shuffling as encoder, and FCN8s [14] as decoder. ENet [18] uses early downsampling of the input to extract relevant image features while reducing the image size. ENet also uses a much smaller decoder module than in typical symmetric encoder-decoder architectures [2,22].

Two-branch networks [19,29] are another way to design faster models and are among the fastest existing methods. Unlike standard models where the entire network learns low-level and high-level details, in two-branch networks these two tasks are performed by two separate branches. A shallow branch captures spatial details and generates high-resolution feature representation, while a deeper but lightweight branch learns high-level semantic context. ContextNet [19], Fast-SCNN [20], and BiseNet [29] are examples of two-branch networks. An important consideration in designing these architectures is to ensure proper integration of high-level and low-level context information. For example, ICNet [31] computes a multi-resolution set of feature maps and employs a cascade feature fusion unit to fuse these feature maps, whereas DFANet [13] uses several interconnected encoding paths to add high-level context into the encoded features.

In this work we aimed to design a network with proper, efficient integration of high-level and low-level information to achieve high accuracy and very fast inference in fetal brain MRI segmentation. To achieve this, we developed a new, efficient CNN-based network, which we term Real-time Fetal Brain Segmenta-tion Network (RFBSNet). RFBSNet uses an encoder-decoder architecture with forward connections to retain accuracy; and a two-branch architecture with an input downsampling module to achieve fast inference. We compared RFBSNet with eight alternative state-of-the-art DL models. In the following sections, we provide a detailed description of our methods, data, results, and analysis.

2   Materials and Methods

2.1   Proposed Network Architecture

We designed RFBSNet to strike a balance between inference speed and accuracy. Figure 1 shows the layout of RFBSNet. It contains an input downsampling module, a feature extractor, a decoder, and a classification module. In the following, we describe each structure module in more detail.

Input Downsampling Module. The first module in our proposed network is a downsampling module that reduces the size of the input image while also providing high resolution spatial information into the classifier module using a forward path. Input downsampling can greatly speed up the network by significantly reducing the amount of computation performed by all down-stream network layers. When this down-sampling is not excessive and is carried out using learnable functions, such as a convolution layer, the loss in segmentation accuracy can be very small. However, excessive down-sampling can result in a loss of important detail such as fine object boundaries [18]. Besides, downsampling the input image by a factor of m would require upsampling by the same factor in order to obtain a segmentation map with the same size as the input image. Although upsampling can also be accomplished using learnable transposed convolutions, it can result in further loss of fine detail if it is excessive. To avoid these negative effects, we used a down-sampling module, shown in Fig. 2, that consists of two paths: (1) a max-pooling path with non-overlapping 2×2 windows, and (2) a convolutional layer with 3×3 kernels. The outputs of these two paths are concatenated.

Feature Extractor. This module is responsible for learning multi-resolution image features for accurate segmentation. Our feature extractor module shares its computation of the first few layers with the input downsampling module. This parameter sharing not only reduces the computational complexity of the network, it also improves the segmentation accuracy. In this architecture, we used one convolutional layer followed by ReLU in the shallow branch to encode detailed spatial information. The deep feature extractor branch of RFBSNet provides sufficient receptive field. We deployed U-Net style [22] forward skip connections to fuse multi-resolution features into the decoder module.

Decoder and Classification Modules. A U-Net-type decoder with skip connections upsamples the features learned by the different sections of the feature extractor module to the size of the feature maps generated by the input downsampling module. These feature maps are finally fused together using a simple

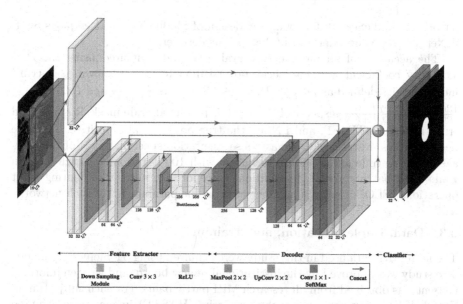

Fig. 1. Overview of the proposed architecture (RFBSNet). It consists of an input downsampling module, a feature extractor, a decoder, and a classifier, with two branches and forward connections from the feature extractor to the decoder. All modules are built using classical convolution layers using operations shown in the figure legend. The detail of the down sampling module is shown in Fig. 2. Numbers next to each block show the number of channels, while the length indicates the spatial size considering the input size of I.

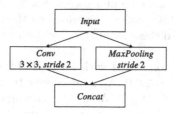

Fig. 2. The input downsampling module in RFBSNet consists of a convolution and a max pooling path. The outputs are concatenated to build a feature map.

addition. In the classification module, an upsampling layer and a pointwise convolution layer are applied to the fused feature maps. A softmax operation is applied to the final layer to generate class probability maps.

2.2   Alternative Methods and Evaluation Metrics

We compare the proposed RFBSNet to two standard networks for medical image segmentation (U-Net [22] and SegNet [2]), as well as several recent architectures that have been proposed for real-time segmentation (see Table 1). We also

introduce ShuffleSeg V2 following the design of ShuffleSeg [5]. It employs ShuffleNet V2 [16] as encoder and FCN8s [14] as decoder.

The accuracy of all methods are evaluated and compared using the Dice
similarity coefficient and Intersection-over-Union IoU, also known as Jaccard
index, metrics defined as $Dice(P,R) = \frac{2|P \cap R|}{|P|+|R|} = \frac{2TP}{2TP+FP+FN}$ and $IoU(P,R) =$
$\frac{|P \cap R|}{|P \cup R|} = \frac{TP}{TP+FP+FN}$ respectively. where P is predicted brain mask, R is a ground
truth mask and TP, FP, and FN are the true positive, false positive, and false
negative rates, respectively. We assess segmentation speed in terms of the average inference time and standard deviation with 100 iterations for each method
while using batch size of 1. In addition, we report the number of floating point
operations (FLOPs) and the number of trainable parameters for each network.

2.3 Data, Implementation, and Training

The fetal MRI data used in this study were acquired using 3T Siemens scanners.
The study was approved by the institutional review board; and written informed
consent was obtained from all research MRI participants. For each subject, multiple half-Fourier single shot turbo spin echo (HASTE) images were acquired
with in-plane resolution of 1 to 1.25 mm, and slice thickness of 2 to 4 mm. The
gestational ages of the fetuses at the time of scans were between 22 to 38 weeks
(mean = 29, stdev = 5). In total, 3496 2D fetal MRI slices (of 131 stacks from 23
fetal MRI sessions) were included in the training and validation procedure (80%
train, 20% validation). A set of 840 2D slices (17 stacks) of two normal fetuses
without severe artifacts was used as normal test set, and a set of 136 2D slices of
a fetal MRI scan with artifacts (from 4 stacks) was used as the challenging test
set. An experienced annotator carefully segmented the fetal brain in every slice
of all these stacks. We used these manual segmentations as the ground truth for
model training and evaluation.

All experiments were conducted with an NVIDIA GeForce RTX 2080 Ti,
using TensorFlow and Keras 2.6.0. All models were trained with a batch size of
8 and input image size of 256 × 256. We used Dice similarity coefficient between
the network predictions and the ground truth as the training loss function. The
learning rate for each of the compared networks was tuned separately. For our
model we used an initial learning rate of 1×10^{-4}, which we multiplied by 0.9
after every 2000 training steps. We trained each model for 100 epochs using
Adam optimization [11] of stochastic gradient descent.

3 Results

Table 1 summarizes the performance of our proposed RFBSNet compared to
other methods. In terms of almost all evaluation criteria, RFBSNet outperformed the standard methods as well as other state-of-the-art real-time segmentation models. It reached 97.99% aDice (average Dice of all test images),
96.12% aIoU on normal and 86.04% aDice, 75.50% aIoU on challenging test sets
with outstanding inference time of 3.36 ms. Indeed, our network can run on a

Table 1. Comparing RFBSNet with eight state-of-the-art methods based on average Dice (aDice) and average IOU (aIoU) on normal and challenging test sets. This table also shows the number of FLOPS (in giga FLOPS), the number of training parameters, and the inference time (in ms) of each method. RFBSNet achieved the highest accuracy and the best inference speed among all methods.

Model	Normal		Challenging		FLOPs (G)	#Trainable Parameters	Inference Time (ms)
	aDice (%)	aIoU (%)	aDice (%)	aIoU (%)			
ICNet [31]	85.43	77.00	65.15	58.00	1.81	6,710,914	12.91±0.39
ENet [18]	95.42	91.54	78.05	69.00	0.975	362,838	20.63±0.05
Fast-SCNN [20]	86.87	78.81	69.34	60.80	0.517	1,593,222	5.74±0.09
DFANet [13]	78.59	69.19	65.47	57.97	0.248	418,354	22.90±0.32
ShuffleSeg [5]	91.34	85.05	79.38	70.35	0.374	940,722	12.05±1.11
ShuffleSeg V2 [16]	89.97	83.05	77.36	68.26	1.15	3,043,294	8.64±0.25
SegNet [2]	96.17	92.85	88.95	81.74	79.9	29,441,986	10.16±0.18
U-Net [22]	97.93	96.02	85.81	77.63	102	34,512,258	9.82±0.04
RFBSNet	**97.99**	**96.12**	**84.04**	**75.50**	**5.32**	**2,154,328**	**3.36±0.02**

single GPU in real time, i.e., it runs as soon as a single MRI slice is acquired and reconstructed. We note that RFBSNet performed better than the standard medical image segmentation network U-Net in terms of both accuracy and speed while having ≈14 times less number of parameters and FLOPs. Our method also outperformed other real-time segmentation methods in both accuracy and speed while representing comparable number of parameters and FLOPs.

We performed paired t-tests with a p value threshold of 0.001 to test if the segmentation accuracy, in terms of Dice and IoU on the test sets, for our model was higher than other models. These tests showed that our model was significantly more accurate than all competing real-time segmentation models on the normal and challenging test images in terms of both Dice and IoU. Our model was also significantly more accurate than SegNet. However, the differences with the U-Net were not statistically significant ($p \approx 0.3$). We note that in addition to computation time, both UNet and SegNet require high GPU memory which may limit their use with larger images on standard GPUs.

Example segmentation results can be seen in Fig. 3. In addition to our own method, in this figure we have shown the results of those competing methods that were proposed originally for real-time segmentation. As these representative examples show, compared to those other methods, which showed large segmentation errors and often completely failed to segment the fetal brain on challenging images, our method accurately segmented both normal and challenging images.

4   Analysis and Discussion

We further analyzed the performance of the networks and the speed-accuracy balance. Figure 4 shows the run-time of different networks, which were implemented and compared in this study, as a function of batch size. The main observation from this figure is the dramatic shift in the order of networks as the batch

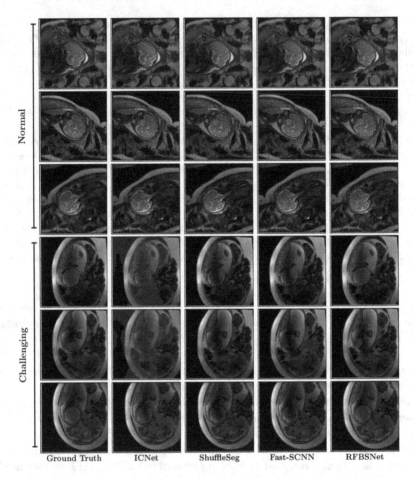

Normal

Challenging

Ground Truth   ICNet   ShuffleSeg   Fast-SCNN   RFBSNet

Fig. 3. Representative examples of predicted brain masks overlaid on original fetal MRI slices for normal cases (top 3 rows) and challenging cases (bottom 3 rows). Note that RFBSNet correctly segmented the brain in all slices of this challenging test case which was not segmented by the other methods.

size decreases. For batch sizes larger than four, real-time segmentation networks were significantly faster than standard networks. However, the order began to reverse as the batch size decreased to 1. At a batch size of 1, the processing time (per image) for all real-time segmentation networks is several times longer than those of the batch size of 10. In fact, four out of the six competing real-time segmentation networks became slower than U-Net and SegNet. Our proposed network, on the other hand, is comparable with other real-time networks for large batches and it is the fastest of all networks for a batch size of 1 (which is used for real-time inference). Figure 5 shows the speed-accuracy trade-off comparison of all methods on the normal test set with the top left corner being the optimal performance.

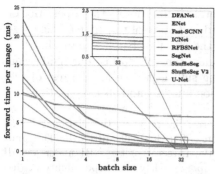

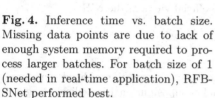

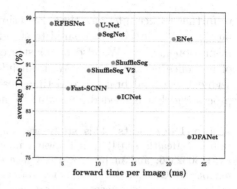

Fig. 4. Inference time vs. batch size. Missing data points are due to lack of enough system memory required to process larger batches. For batch size of 1 (needed in real-time application), RFB-SNet performed best.

Fig. 5. Inference time vs. average Dice coefficient. This chart shows the speed-accuracy trade-off comparison on the test set at batch size of 1 for all methods that were implemented and compared in this study.

By design, our proposed network (RFBSNet) achieved high accuracy and very fast inference at batch size of 1 for real-time image segmentation. The learnable input downsampling module in RFBSNet helped reduce the computations while providing a capacity to learn full spatial image resolution details. This module resembled the shallow spatial path [20] of two-branch models [19]. Our feature extractor module, on the other hand, can be compared to the deep low-resolution branch of those prior works. This module helped ensure a high segmentation accuracy.

As explained in Sect. 1, depthwise-separable convolutions (DWSConv) [7] are a common design choice for reducing the computational cost of DL models. However, because DWSConv involves far fewer floating point operations than standard 2D convolutions, its execution time on a GPU is dominated by the memory access latency [15]. To overcome this bottleneck, existing implementations of DWSConv try to accelerate execution by using large batch sizes. However, this strategy does not work in applications where inference is highly latency-sensitive and when smaller batch sizes have to be used. Hence, DWS-Convs does not result in fast models in a real-time application such as fetal brain segmentation, where a test-time batch size of one is desired.

5   Conclusion

In this paper, we proposed a fast and accurate CNN based network for fetal brain segmentation in MRI. Our design combines spatial details at high resolution with context features extracted at lower resolutions. We also used multiple branches with skip connections to maintain high accuracy while devising a parallel combination of convolution and pooling operations as an input down-sampling module to further reduce inference time. Experimental results showed the superiority of our proposed network compared to standard and state-of-the-art real-time segmentation models. We also demonstrated the effect of batch size at the time of inference on the latency. With an inference time of <5 ms, our model can segment the fetal brain in real time, leaving sufficient time for the rest of the processing that is needed for real-time motion analysis and slice navigation.

Acknowledgements. This study was supported in part by the National Institutes of Health (NIH) under award numbers R01EB031849, R01NS106030, and R01EB032366; and in part by the Office of the Director of the NIH under award number S10OD0250111. The content of this paper is solely the responsibility of the authors and does not necessarily represent the official views of the NIH.

References

1. Anquez, J., Angelini, E.D., Bloch, I.: Automatic segmentation of head structures on fetal MRI. In: 2009 IEEE International Symposium on Biomedical Imaging: From Nano to Macro, pp. 109–112. IEEE (2009)
2. Badrinarayanan, V., Kendall, A., Cipolla, R.: SegNet: a deep convolutional encoder-decoder architecture for image segmentation. IEEE Trans. Pattern Anal. Mach. Intell. **39**(12), 2481–2495 (2017)
3. Ebner, M., et al.: An automated localization, segmentation and reconstruction framework for fetal brain MRI. In: Frangi, A.F., Schnabel, J.A., Davatzikos, C., Alberola-López, C., Fichtinger, G. (eds.) MICCAI 2018. LNCS, vol. 11070, pp. 313–320. Springer, Cham (2018). https://doi.org/10.1007/978-3-030-00928-1_36
4. Ebner, M., et al.: An automated framework for localization, segmentation and super-resolution reconstruction of fetal brain MRI. Neuroimage **206**, 116324 (2020)
5. Gamal, M., Siam, M., Abdel-Razek, M.: ShuffleSeg: real-time semantic segmentation network. arXiv preprint arXiv:1803.03816 (2018)
6. Gholipour, A., Estroff, J.A., Warfield, S.K.: Robust super-resolution volume reconstruction from slice acquisitions: application to fetal brain MRI. IEEE Trans. Med. Imaging **29**(10), 1739–1758 (2010)
7. Howard, A.G., et al.: MobileNets: efficient convolutional neural networks for mobile vision applications. arXiv preprint arXiv:1704.04861 (2017)
8. Kainz, B., et al.: Fast volume reconstruction from motion corrupted stacks of 2D slices. IEEE Trans. Med. Imaging **34**(9), 1901–1913 (2015)
9. Keraudren, K., et al.: Automated fetal brain segmentation from 2D MRI slices for motion correction. Neuroimage **101**, 633–643 (2014)
10. Khalili, N., et al.: Automatic segmentation of the intracranial volume in fetal MR images. In: Cardoso, M.J., et al. (eds.) FIFI/OMIA -2017. LNCS, vol. 10554, pp. 42–51. Springer, Cham (2017). https://doi.org/10.1007/978-3-319-67561-9_5
11. Kingma, D.P., Ba, J.: Adam: a method for stochastic optimization. arXiv preprint arXiv:1412.6980 (2014)
12. Kuklisova-Murgasova, M., Quaghebeur, G., Rutherford, M.A., Hajnal, J.V., Schnabel, J.A.: Reconstruction of fetal brain MRI with intensity matching and complete outlier removal. Med. Image Anal. **16**(8), 1550–1564 (2012)
13. Li, H., Xiong, P., Fan, H., Sun, J.: DFANet: deep feature aggregation for real-time semantic segmentation. In: Proceedings of the IEEE/CVF Conference on Computer Vision and Pattern Recognition, pp. 9522–9531 (2019)

14. Long, J., Shelhamer, E., Darrell, T.: Fully convolutional networks for semantic segmentation. In: Proceedings of the IEEE Conference on Computer Vision and Pattern Recognition, pp. 3431–3440 (2015)
15. Lu, G., Zhang, W., Wang, Z.: Optimizing depthwise separable convolution operations on GPUs. IEEE Trans. Parallel Distrib. Syst. **33**(1), 70–87 (2021)
16. Ma, N., Zhang, X., Zheng, H.-T., Sun, J.: ShuffleNet V2: practical guidelines for efficient CNN architecture design. In: Ferrari, V., Hebert, M., Sminchisescu, C., Weiss, Y. (eds.) Computer Vision – ECCV 2018. LNCS, vol. 11218, pp. 122–138. Springer, Cham (2018). https://doi.org/10.1007/978-3-030-01264-9_8
17. Papadeas, I., Tsochatzidis, L., Amanatiadis, A., Pratikakis, I.: Real-time semantic image segmentation with deep learning for autonomous driving: a survey. Appl. Sci. **11**(19), 8802 (2021)
18. Paszke, A., Chaurasia, A., Kim, S., Culurciello, E.: ENet: a deep neural network architecture for real-time semantic segmentation. arXiv preprint arXiv:1606.02147 (2016)
19. Poudel, R.P., Bonde, U., Liwicki, S., Zach, C.: ContextNet: exploring context and detail for semantic segmentation in real-time. arXiv preprint arXiv:1805.04554 (2018)
20. Poudel, R.P., Liwicki, S., Cipolla, R.: Fast-SCNN: fast semantic segmentation network. In: British Machine Vision Conference (2019)
21. Rampun, A., Jarvis, D., Griffiths, P., Armitage, P.: Automated 2D fetal brain segmentation of MR images using a deep U-Net. In: Palaiahnakote, S., Sanniti di Baja, G., Wang, L., Yan, W.Q. (eds.) ACPR 2019. LNCS, vol. 12047, pp. 373–386. Springer, Cham (2020). https://doi.org/10.1007/978-3-030-41299-9_29
22. Ronneberger, O., Fischer, P., Brox, T.: U-Net: convolutional networks for biomedical image segmentation. In: Navab, N., Hornegger, J., Wells, W.M., Frangi, A.F. (eds.) MICCAI 2015. LNCS, vol. 9351, pp. 234–241. Springer, Cham (2015). https://doi.org/10.1007/978-3-319-24574-4_28
23. Salehi, S.S.M., Erdogmus, D., Gholipour, A.: Auto-context convolutional neural network (auto-net) for brain extraction in magnetic resonance imaging. IEEE Trans. Med. Imaging **36**(11), 2319–2330 (2017)
24. Salehi, S.S.M., et al.: Real-time automatic fetal brain extraction in fetal MRI by deep learning. In: 2018 IEEE 15th International Symposium on Biomedical Imaging (ISBI 2018), pp. 720–724. IEEE (2018)
25. Salehi, S.S.M., Khan, S., Erdogmus, D., Gholipour, A.: Real-time deep pose estimation with geodesic loss for image-to-template rigid registration. IEEE Trans. Med. Imaging **38**(2), 470–481 (2018)
26. Uus, A., et al.: Deformable slice-to-volume registration for motion correction of fetal body and placenta MRI. IEEE Trans. Med. Imaging **39**(9), 2750–2759 (2020)
27. Wang, G., Aertsen, M., Deprest, J., Ourselin, S., Vercauteren, T., Zhang, S.: Uncertainty-guided efficient interactive refinement of fetal brain segmentation from stacks of MRI slices. In: Martel, A.L., et al. (eds.) MICCAI 2020. LNCS, vol. 12264, pp. 279–288. Springer, Cham (2020). https://doi.org/10.1007/978-3-030-59719-1_28
28. Wang, G., Li, W., Aertsen, M., Deprest, J., Ourselin, S., Vercauteren, T.: Aleatoric uncertainty estimation with test-time augmentation for medical image segmentation with convolutional neural networks. Neurocomputing **338**, 34–45 (2019)
29. Yu, C., Wang, J., Peng, C., Gao, C., Yu, G., Sang, N.: BiSeNet: bilateral segmentation network for real-time semantic segmentation. In: Ferrari, V., Hebert, M., Sminchisescu, C., Weiss, Y. (eds.) ECCV 2018. LNCS, vol. 11217, pp. 334–349. Springer, Cham (2018). https://doi.org/10.1007/978-3-030-01261-8_20

30. Zhang, X., Zhou, X., Lin, M., Sun, J.: ShuffleNet: an extremely efficient convolutional neural network for mobile devices. In: Proceedings of the IEEE Conference on Computer Vision and Pattern Recognition, pp. 6848–6856 (2018)
31. Zhao, H., Qi, X., Shen, X., Shi, J., Jia, J.: ICNet for real-time semantic segmentation on high-resolution images. In: Ferrari, V., Hebert, M., Sminchisescu, C., Weiss, Y. (eds.) ECCV 2018. LNCS, vol. 11207, pp. 418–434. Springer, Cham (2018). https://doi.org/10.1007/978-3-030-01219-9_25

Attention-Driven Multi-channel Deformable Registration of Structural and Microstructural Neonatal Data

Irina Grigorescu[1,2]($\boxtimes$), Alena Uus[1,2], Daan Christiaens[1,3],
Lucilio Cordero-Grande[1,2,5], Jana Hutter[1], Dafnis Batalle[1,4],
A. David Edwards[1], Joseph V. Hajnal[1,2], Marc Modat[2], and Maria Deprez[1,2]

[1] Centre for the Developing Brain, School of Biomedical Engineering
and Imaging Sciences, King's College London, London, UK
`irina.grigorescu@kcl.ac.uk`
[2] Biomedical Engineering Department, School of Biomedical Engineering
and Imaging Sciences, King's College London, London, UK
[3] Departments of Electrical Engineering, ESAT/PSI, KU Leuven, Leuven, Belgium
[4] Department of Forensic and Neurodevelopmental Science, Institute of Psychiatry,
Psychology and Neuroscience, King's College London, London, UK
[5] Biomedical Image Technologies, ETSI Telecomunicación, Universidad Politécnica
de Madrid & CIBER-BNN, Madrid, Spain

Abstract. Image registration of structural and microstructural data allows accurate alignment of anatomical and diffusion channels. However, existing techniques employ simple fusion-based approaches, which use a global weight for each modality, or empirically-driven approaches, which rely on pre-calculated local certainty maps. Here, we present a novel attention-based deep learning deformable image registration solution for aligning multi-channel neonatal MRI data. We learn optimal attention maps to weigh each modality-specific velocity field in a spatially varying fashion, thus allowing for local fusion of structural and microstructural images. We evaluate our proposed method on registrations of 30 multi-channel neonatal MRI to a standard structural and microstructural atlas, and compare it against models trained without the use of attention maps on either single or both modalities. We show that by combining the two channels through attention-driven image registration, we take full advantage of the two complementary modalities, and achieve the best overall alignment of both structural and microstructural data.

Keywords: multi-channel registration · attention maps · deep learning registration

1 Introduction

The neonatal brain undergoes dramatic changes during early life, such as cortical folding and myelination. Non-invasive magnetic resonance imaging (MRI) offers

R. Licandro et al. (Eds.): PIPPI 2022, LNCS 13575, pp. 71–81, 2022.
https://doi.org/10.1007/978-3-031-17117-8_7

snapshots of the evolving morphology and tissue properties in developing brain across multiple subjects and time-points. As a prerequisite of further analysis, MRI of various modalities needs to be aligned. Structural and microstructural MRI modalities offer complementary information about morphology and tissue properties of the developing brain, however inter-subject alignment is most commonly driven by a single modality (structural [2] or diffusion [23]). Studies have shown that combining diffusion and structural data to drive the registration [1,7,8,20] improves the overall alignment. Classic approaches for fusing these channels are based on simple averaging of the deformation fields from the individual channels [1], or weighting the deformation fields based on certainty maps calculated from normalised gradients correlated to structural content [7,19,20].

In order to establish accurate correspondences between MR images acquired during the neonatal period, we propose an attention-driven multi-channel deep learning image registration framework that aims to combine information from T_2-weighted (T_2w) neonatal scans with diffusion weighted imaging (DWI)-derived fractional anisotropy (FA) maps. Our proposed solution selects the most salient features from these 2 image modalities to improve alignment of individual MRI images to a common atlas space.

More specifically, we train conditional variational autoencoder (CVAE) image registration networks to align either structural or microstructural data to 36 weeks neonatal atlas [19] of the same modality. As a second step, we build a convolutional neural network (CNN) which learns attention maps for weighted combination of the predicted modality-specific velocity fields to achieve an optimal multi-channel alignment. Throughout this work, we use 3-D MRI brain scans [6] acquired as part of the developing Human Connectome Project (dHCP[1] as the moving images, and 36 weeks neonatal multi-modal atlas[2] [19] as the fixed image.

We evaluate our proposed framework on a test set of 30 neonates scanned around 40 weeks post-menstrual age (PMA), and we compare the results against registration networks trained on T_2w-only, FA-only, and both modalities at the same time, either without attention, or with previously proposed attention mechanism [9,21]. The quantitative evaluation confirmed that while cortical structures were better aligned using T_2w data and white matter tracts were better aligned using FA maps, the attention-based multi-channel registration aligned both types of structures accurately.

2   Method

Image Registration Network. In this study, we employ a CVAE [11] to model the registration probabilistically as proposed by [12]. In short, a pair of 3D MRI volumes M_{T2w} and F_{T2w} (or M_{FA} and F_{FA}) are passed through the network to learn a velocity field v_{T2w} (or v_{FA}). The *exponentiation layers* (with 4 *scaling-and-squaring* [3] steps) transform it into a topology-preserving deformation field

---

[1] developingconnectome.org.

[2] gin.g-node.org/alenaullauus/4d_multi-channel_neonatal_brain_mri_atlas.

ϕ_{T2w} (or ϕ_{FA}). A *Spatial Transformer* layer [5] is then used to warp (linearly resample) the moving images M_{T2w} (or M_{FA}) and obtain the moved image $M_{T2w}(\phi_{T2w})$ (or $M_{FA}(\phi_{FA})$). We keep the network architecture similar to the original paper [12], but use a latent code size of 32 and a Gaussian smoothing layer with $\sigma = 1$ mm (kernel size 3^3). Throughout this work, we use 36 weeks old neonatal structural (T_2w) and microstructural (FA maps) atlases [19] as the fixed images. We have chosen this age for the templates due to the lower degree of gyrification which facilitates a more accurate registration of the cortex across the cohort.

Attention Image Registration Network. We construct a CNN which uses pairs of modality-specific velocity fields as an input, and outputs a combined velocity field which aims to align both structural and microstructural data simultaneously. The network learns the attention maps α_{T2w} and α_{FA}, for which $\alpha_{T2w} + \alpha_{FA} = 1$ at every voxel. The input velocity fields are weighted with the attention maps and combined to create a final velocity field v.

The architecture of our proposed *attention image registration network* is presented in Fig. 1. For each subject in our dataset, we employ the previously trained *registration-only networks* on either pairs of T_2w images (M_{T2w} and F_{T2w}) or FA maps (M_{FA} and F_{FA}) to output modality-specific velocity fields v_{T2w} and v_{FA}. These two fields are concatenated and put through three 3D convolutional layers (stride 2) of 16, 32, and 64 filters, respectively, with a kernel size of 3^3, followed by *Leaky ReLU* ($\alpha = 0.2$) activations [22]. The activation maps of the final layer are concatenated with the subject's moving images M_{T2w} and M_{FA} downsampled to size 16^3. This is followed by three 3D convolutional layers (stride 1) of 32, 16, and 16 filters, respectively, with a kernel size of 3^3, *Leaky ReLU* ($\alpha = 0.2$) activations and upsampling. The final two layers are: one 3D convolutional layer (with stride 1, 8 filters, and *Leaky ReLU* activation), and one 3D convolutional layer (with stride 1, and 2 filters), followed by a *Softmax* activation function which outputs the two modality-specific attention maps α_{T2w} and α_{FA}. The final velocity field is created as $v = v_{T2w} \odot \alpha_{T2w} + v_{FA} \odot \alpha_{FA}$, where $\odot$ represents element-wise multiplication. Similar to the registration network, the velocity field v is put through an *exponentiation layer* to create the combined field ϕ, which is then used to warp the moving volumes M_{T2w} and M_{FA}.

Channel and Spatial Attention Network. To compare our proposed attention-driven image registration network with other attention techniques, we add channel and spatial attention modules throughout the image registration network. More specifically, after every convolutional layer of the network, we add a channel attention module (squeeze-and-excitation block [9]), followed by a spatial attention module [21]. In total, we add 4 channel+spatial attention modules in the encoder part of the CVAE, and 5 modules in the decoder.

Loss Functions. For this study, we train the *registration-only network* and the *channel+spatial attention network* using the following loss function:

$$\mathcal{L}_{reg} = \mathcal{L}_{KLD} + \lambda \left(\lambda_{T2w} \mathcal{L}_{NCC}^{T2w} + \lambda_{FA} \mathcal{L}_{NCC}^{FA} \right) + \lambda_{reg} \mathcal{L}_{BE} \tag{1}$$

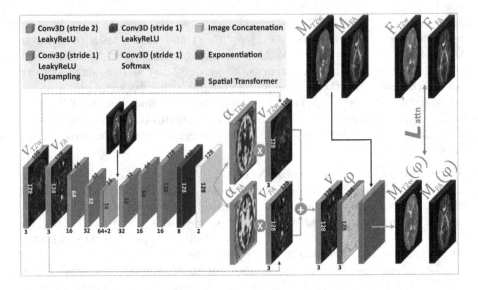

Fig. 1. Our proposed attention-based image registration network architecture, which uses as input subject- and modality-specific velocity fields (v_{T2w} and v_{FA}). The attention network outputs two 1-channel maps α_{T2w} and α_{FA} which are used to create a combined velocity field v. The velocity field v is transformed into a dense displacement field ϕ which warps the subject's moving images (M_{T2w} and M_{FA}) into $M_{T2w}(\phi)$ and $M_{FA}(\phi)$. The network is trained to achieve good alignment between the warped images and the fixed atlases (F_{T2w} and F_{FA}).

and our proposed *attention network* with:

$$\mathcal{L}_{attn} = \lambda_{T2w}\,\mathcal{L}_{NCC}^{T2w} + \lambda_{FA}\,\mathcal{L}_{NCC}^{FA} \qquad (2)$$

where λ, λ_{reg}, λ_{T2w} and λ_{FA} are hyperparameters, $\mathcal{L}_{KLD}$ is the Kullback-Leibler (KL) divergence, $\mathcal{L}_{NCC}$ is the global symmetric normalised cross correlation (NCC) dissimilarity measure, and $\mathcal{L}_{BE}$ is a bending energy regularisation penalty [16]. In this study, we set $\lambda_{reg} = 0.01$ and $\lambda = 5000$ (as proposed in [12]).

Training. First, using the no-attention *registration-only network*, we train 2 single-modality models on either pairs of T_2w-only data ($\lambda_{T2w} = 1.0$, $\lambda_{FA} = 0.0$) or FA-only data ($\lambda_{T2w} = 0.0$, $\lambda_{FA} = 1.0$). Then, we train the three networks (the no-attention *registration-only network*, the *channel+spatial attention network*, and our proposed *attention network*) on both modalities, using the following sets of hyperparameters: $(\lambda_{T2w}, \lambda_{FA}) = \{(1.0, 0.1), (1.0, 0.175), (1.0, 0.25), (1.0, 0.5), (1.0, 0.75), (1.0, 1.0)\}$. In total, we have 20 models: 8 using the *registration-only network*, 6 using the *channel+spatial attention network*, and 6 with our proposed *attention network*.

We train the 20 models until convergence (150 epochs, or 52500 iterations), using the Adam optimizer with its default parameters ($\beta_1 = .9$ and $\beta_2 = .999$), a decaying cyclical learning rate scheduler [17] with a base learning rate of 10^{-6}

and a maximum learning rate of 10^{-3}, and an L_2 weight decay factor of 10^{-5}. All networks were implemented in PyTorch (v1.10.2), with TorchIO (v0.18.73) [15] for data preprocessing (intensity normalisation) and loading, and training was performed on a 12 GB Titan XP. Average inference times were: 0.16 s/sample for the *registration-only networks*, 0.31 s/sample for the *attention-based networks*, and 0.63 s/sample for the *channel+spatial attention networks*.

3 Results

Image Selection and Preprocessing For this study, we use a total of 414 T_2w images and FA maps of neonates born between 23–42 weeks gestational age (GA) and scanned at term-equivalent age (37–45 weeks PMA) [6]. As preprocessing steps, we first affinely pre-registered the data to a common 36 weeks gestational age atlas space [19] using the MIRTK software toolbox [16], and then we resampled both structural and microstructural volumes to be 1 mm isotropic resolution. To obtain the FA maps, we used the MRtrix3 toolbox [18], and we performed skull-stripping using the available dHCP brain masks [4]. Finally, we cropped the resulting images to a $128 \times 128 \times 128$ size.

Out of the 414 subjects in our dataset, we used 350 for training, 34 for validation and 30 subjects for test, as described in Table 1. We used the validation set to inform us about our models' performance during training, and we report all of our results on the test set.

Table 1. Number of scans in different datasets used for training, validation and testing the models, together with their mean GA at birth (standard deviation) and mean PMA at scan (standard deviation).

Dataset	#Subjects	GA [weeks]	PMA [weeks]
Train	350 (164♀ + 186♂)	38.0 (3.8)	40.6 (1.9)
Validate	34 (14♀ + 20♂)	39.7 (1.4)	40.7 (1.7)
Test	30 (12♀ + 18♂)	39.8 (1.5)	40.6 (1.9)

Quantitative Evaluation. To validate which of the 20 models performs best, we carry out a quantitative evaluation on our test dataset of 30 subjects. Each subject and the atlas had the following tissue label segmentations obtained from T_2w images using the Draw-EM pipeline [14]: cortical gray matter (cGM), white matter (WM), ventricles, hippocampi and amygdala. Additionally, a WM structure called the internal capsule (IC) was manually segmented on FA maps of all test subjects. These labels were propagated from each subject into the atlas space using the predicted deformation fields. To evaluate performance of the registration, Dice scores and average surface distances (SimpleITK v2.1.1 [13]) were calculated between the warped labels and the atlas labels.

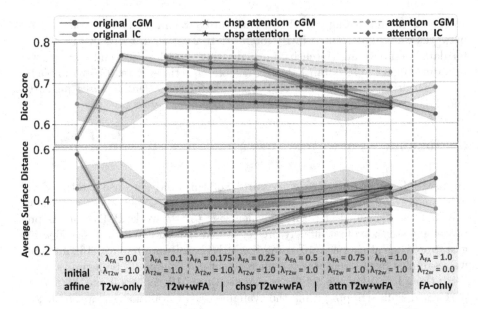

Fig. 2. Line plots showing median Dice scores (first row) and average surface distances (second row) for cGM and IC structures, with the first column showing their initial affine alignment. The dark blue lines (*original cGM*) and the orange lines (*original IC*) show the scores for the registration models without attention. The light blue (*attention cGM*) and the red (*attention IC*) plots represent the values obtained by our *proposed attention-driven image registration network*, while the green (*chsp attention cGM*) and the brown (*chsp attention IC*) lines represent the values obtained by the *channel+spatial attention network*, for different values of the λ_{T2w} and λ_{FA} hyperparameters. The shading around each median line is the IQR. (Color figure online)

First, we looked at how the models performed based on two tissue types (the cGM and the IC). We chose these structures because the cGM delineation is poor on the FA maps, while the IC is a white matter structure which is very prominent in the microstructure data. Both Dice scores and average surface distances are summarised in Fig. 2, where the first column shows the values for the initial affine alignment, while the second and last columns show the T_2w-only and the FA-only image registration networks. Columns 3–8 show different multi-channel models for increasing values of the λ_{FA} hyperparameter, while λ_{T2w} is kept the same.

The best overall performance in terms of Dice scores and average surface distances is obtained by our *proposed attention model* for $\lambda_{T2w} = 1.0$ and $\lambda_{FA} = 0.1$ (third column, Fig. 2), where the cGM is aligned as well as the T_2w-*only* model, and the IC structure as good as the FA-only model (the differences are not statistically significant). Using *channel+spatial attention* with the same hyperparameter setup ($\lambda_{T2w} = 1.0$ and $\lambda_{FA} = 0.1$) achieves good results for the cGM structure, but cannot align the IC structure as well as the FA-only model, or the *proposed attention model*.

For the T_2w-only model (second column) the IC is poorly aligned, obtaining scores which are worse than the initial affine alignment, while the cGM label obtains the best alignment. On the other hand, for the FA-only model (last column) the IC is well aligned, while the cGM obtains lower scores. In the original registration networks (dark blue and orange) we see a steady worsening of cGM scores as λ_{FA} increases, while the IC structure varies across the different λ_{FA} values. For the attention-driven networks (light blue and red), the scores in cGM degrade more gently, while the IC structures remain steady. Finally, the proposed attention networks always outperform the multi-channel registration networks with no attention, and this improvement is statistically significant for all values of λ_{FA}.

Table 2 shows the results of 6 of our trained models for all tissue types (cGM, WM, ventricles, hippocampi and amygdala, and IC). Here, we call the T_2w + wFA, the *chsp* T_2w + wFA, and the *attn* T_2w + wFA models as the ones trained with the lowest weight on the FA maps ($\lambda_{T2w} = 1.0$ and $\lambda_{FA} = 0.1$).

Table 2. Mean (±standard deviation) Dice scores (DS) and average surface distances (ASD) on test set. Best scores are highlighted in bold (*t-test* $p < 0.05$), while the green shading highlights the model which performed best amongst the ones which use both T_2w and FA modalities (*t-test* $p < 0.05$). The multi-modality weighted models shown here use $\lambda_{T2w} = 1.0$ and $\lambda_{FA} = 0.1$.

Model	cGM	WM	Ventricles	Amygdala	IC	
affine	.567±.02	.7±.03	.631±.05	.746±.05	.642±.07	
T2w-only	**.763±.01**	**.844±.02**	**.797±.02**	.803±.02	.614±.04	
FA-only	.621±.02	.756±.02	.676±.04	.769±.03	**.686±.03**	DS
T2w+FA	.653±.01	.766±.01	.742±.03	.782±.02	.655±.03	
T2w+wFA	.747±.01	.826±.02	.775±.02	.808±.02	.669±.03	
chsp T2w+wFA	.761±.01	.841±.01	.791±.01	**.814±.02**	.656±.03	
attn T2w+wFA	**.763±.01**	.842±.01	.793±.02	**.816±.02**	**.683±.03**	
affine	.582±.04	.409±.04	.508±.1	.31±.08	.479±.1	
T2w-only	**.259±.02**	**.193±.02**	**.242±.05**	.233±.04	.498±.09	
FA-only	.477±.04	.319±.02	.433±.09	.276±.05	**.374±.05**	ASD
T2w+FA	.419±.02	.317±.02	.324±.06	.266±.04	.417±.06	
T2w+wFA	.279±.01	.218±.02	.264±.04	.223±.04	.383±.05	
chsp T2w+wFA	**.262±.01**	.198±.01	.248±.04	**.209±.03**	.39±.05	
attn T2w+wFA	**.260±.02**	.197±.01	.248±.04	**.212±.03**	**.37±.05**	

Our proposed *attn* T_2w + wFA model has the best overall performance. For structures which were delineated in T_2w images, the proposed attention model performed better (hippocampi and amygdala), equally well (cGM), or very close (WM, ventricles) to the T_2w-*only* model, showing that thanks to attention we are able to keep advantages of structural only registration. For IC, which was derived from FA maps, the proposed attention model performed equally well to the *FA-only* model, showing that the attention also allows us to keep the advantages of the microstructural only registration model.

Using *channel+spatial attention* helped with the alignment of the structural labels (cGM, WM, ventricles, hippocampi and amygdala), but had significantly lower performance for IC (lower than the no-attention T_2w+**w**FA model).

The T_2w-*only* model performed slightly worse for the hippocampi and amygdala, while the scores for the IC structure were worse than the initial affine alignment. The *FA-only* model obtains poor scores in all structures except the IC. Finally, the multi-channel models trained without attention always performed worse than the attention-driven models. In fact, the T_2w+*FA* network, where $\lambda_{T2w} = \lambda_{FA} = 1.0$, obtained the lowest performance amongst the multi-channel models, showing that besides attention, the global weighting ($\lambda_{FA} = 0.1$) was an important factor towards the network's performance.

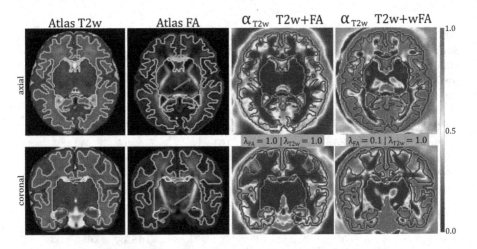

Fig. 3. Mid-brain axial and coronal slices of both T_2w and FA fixed images (first two columns), together with average α_{T2w} attention maps for the *attn* T_2w+*FA* with $\lambda_{FA} = \lambda_{T2w} = 1.0$, and the *attn* T_2w + *w*FA with $\lambda_{T2w} = 1.0$, $\lambda_{FA} = 0.1$ models on the last two columns. Contour lines of the boundaries between cGM (dark blue), WM (cyan), ventricles (yellow) and hippocampi and amygdala (red) are overlaid on top, while the pink arrow points to the IC structure. (Color figure online)

Visualisation of Attention Maps. Figure 3 shows average attention maps from 10 neonatal subjects scanned around 40 weeks PMA for two of our attention-driven models: *attn* T_2w+*FA* ($\lambda_{FA} = \lambda_{T2w} = 1.0$) and *attn* T_2w+*w*FA ($\lambda_{T2w} = 1.0$, $\lambda_{FA} = 0.1$). The first two columns show the middle axial and coronal slices of the T_2w and FA atlases which were used for training, together with segmentation of the investigated brain structures. The last two columns show the average α_{T2w} attention maps (in atlas space) for the 2 models. We can observe that the α_{T2w} attention maps cover the cGM region, and this is more pronounced when λ_{FA} is decreased from 1.0 to 0.1. On the other hand, α_{T2w} is close to zero in the area of the main white matter tracts in both cases.

4   Conclusion

This paper presents a novel solution for multi-channel registration, which combines structural and microstructural MRI data based on learned spatially varying attention maps that optimise the multi-channel alignment. Our quantitative evaluation showed that the proposed attention-driven image registration network improves overall alignment when compared to models trained on multi-channel data, while maintaining the performance of the single-channel registration for the structures delineated on that channel. Moreover, using attention helps drive the registration to better alignment of tissue structures, but only our proposed model obtains results on par to using microstructural data only in terms of aligning white matter labels.

The main limitations of this work are: the use of a single latent code size and smoothing kernel, no comparison with classic multi-channel image registration tools [10,19], and a limited number of labels used for validation. Future work will focus on evaluating the effect of the latent code size and smoothing kernel on the predicted velocity fields, and exploring the use of older neonate atlases. Moreover, we aim to extend our attention-driven image registration network to incorporate higher-order data, such as diffusion tensor (DT) images [8].

Acknowledgements. This work was supported by the Academy of Medical Sciences Springboard Award [SBF004\1040], Medical Research Council (Grant no. [MR/K006355/1]), European Research Council under the European Union's Seventh Framework Programme [FP7/20072013]/ERC grant agreement no. 319456 dHCP project, the EPSRC Research Council as part of the EPSRC DTP (grant Ref: [EP/R513064/1]), the Wellcome/EPSRC Centre for Medical Engineering at King's College London [WT 203148/Z/16/Z], the NIHR Clinical Research Facility (CRF) at Guy's and St Thomas', and by the National Institute for Health Research Biomedical Research Centre based at Guy's and St Thomas' NHS Foundation Trust and King's College London.

References

1. Avants, B., Duda, J.T., Zhang, H., Gee, J.C.: Multivariate normalization with symmetric diffeomorphisms for multivariate studies. In: Ayache, N., Ourselin, S., Maeder, A. (eds.) MICCAI 2007. LNCS, vol. 4791, pp. 359–366. Springer, Heidelberg (2007). https://doi.org/10.1007/978-3-540-75757-3_44
2. Avants, B.B., Epstein, C.L., Grossman, M., Gee, J.C.: Symmetric diffeomorphic image registration with cross-correlation: evaluating automated labeling of elderly and neurodegenerative brain. Med. Image Anal. **12**(1), 26–41 (2008)
3. Balakrishnan, G., Zhao, A., Sabuncu, M.R., Guttag, J., Dalca, A.V.: VoxelMorph: a learning framework for deformable medical image registration. IEEE Trans. Med. Imaging **38**(8), 1788–1800 (2019)

4. Christiaens, D., et al.: Scattered slice SHARD reconstruction for motion correction in multi-shell diffusion MRI. Neuroimage **225**, 117437 (2021)

5. Dalca, A.V., Balakrishnan, G., Guttag, J., Sabuncu, M.R.: Unsupervised learning for fast probabilistic diffeomorphic registration. In: Frangi, A.F., Schnabel, J.A., Davatzikos, C., Alberola-López, C., Fichtinger, G. (eds.) MICCAI 2018. LNCS, vol. 11070, pp. 729–738. Springer, Cham (2018). https://doi.org/10.1007/978-3-030-00928-1_82

6. Edwards, A.D., et al.: The developing human connectome project neonatal data release. Front. Neurosci. **16**, 886772 (2022)

7. Forsberg, D., Rathi, Y., Bouix, S., Wassermann, D., Knutsson, H., Westin, C.-F.: Improving registration using multi-channel diffeomorphic demons combined with certainty maps. In: Liu, T., Shen, D., Ibanez, L., Tao, X. (eds.) MBIA 2011. LNCS, vol. 7012, pp. 19–26. Springer, Heidelberg (2011). https://doi.org/10.1007/978-3-642-24446-9_3

8. Grigorescu, I., et al.: Diffusion tensor driven image registration: a deep learning approach. In: Špiclin, Ž, McClelland, J., Kybic, J., Goksel, O. (eds.) WBIR 2020. LNCS, vol. 12120, pp. 131–140. Springer, Cham (2020). https://doi.org/10.1007/978-3-030-50120-4_13

9. Hu, J., Shen, L., Sun, G.: Squeeze-and-excitation networks. In: Proceedings of the IEEE Conference on Computer Vision and Pattern Recognition, pp. 7132–7141 (2018)

10. Irfanoglu, M.O., et al.: DR-TAMAS: diffeomorphic registration for tensor accurate alignment of anatomical structures. Neuroimage **132**, 439–454 (2016)

11. Kingma, D.P., Rezende, D.J., Mohamed, S., Welling, M.: Semi-supervised learning with deep generative models (2014). arXiv:1406.5298

12. Krebs, J., Mansi, T., Mailhé, B., Ayache, N., Delingette, H.: Unsupervised probabilistic deformation modeling for robust diffeomorphic registration. In: Stoyanov, D., et al. (eds.) DLMIA/ML-CDS -2018. LNCS, vol. 11045, pp. 101–109. Springer, Cham (2018). https://doi.org/10.1007/978-3-030-00889-5_12

13. Lowekamp, B., Chen, D., Ibanez, L., Blezek, D.: The design of SimpleiTK. Front. Neuroinform. **7**, 45 (2013)

14. Makropoulos, A., et al.: Automatic whole brain MRI segmentation of the developing neonatal brain. IEEE Trans. Med. Imaging **33**(9), 1818–1831 (2014)

15. Pérez-García, F., Sparks, R., Ourselin, S.: TorchIO: a Python library for efficient loading, preprocessing, augmentation and patch-based sampling of medical images in deep learning. Comput. Methods Programs Biomed. **208**, 106236 (2021)

16. Rueckert, D., Sonoda, L.I., Hayes, C., Hill, D.L.G., Leach, M.O., Hawkes, D.J.: Nonrigid registration using free-form deformations: application to breast MR images. IEEE Trans. Med. Imaging **18**(8), 712–721 (1999)

17. Smith, L.N.: Cyclical learning rates for training neural networks (2015)

18. Tournier, J.D., et al.: MRtrix3: a fast, flexible and open software framework for medical image processing and visualisation. Neuroimage **202**, 116137 (2019)

19. Uus, A., et al.: Multi-channel 4D parametrized atlas of macro- and microstructural neonatal brain development. Front. Neurosci. **15**, 721 (2021)

20. Uus, A., et al.: Multi-channel registration for diffusion MRI: longitudinal analysis for the neonatal brain. In: Špiclin, Ž, McClelland, J., Kybic, J., Goksel, O. (eds.) WBIR 2020. LNCS, vol. 12120, pp. 111–121. Springer, Cham (2020). https://doi.org/10.1007/978-3-030-50120-4_11

21. Woo, S., Park, J., Lee, J.-Y., Kweon, I.S.: CBAM: convolutional block attention module. In: Ferrari, V., Hebert, M., Sminchisescu, C., Weiss, Y. (eds.) ECCV 2018.

LNCS, vol. 11211, pp. 3–19. Springer, Cham (2018). https://doi.org/10.1007/978-3-030-01234-2_1

22. Xu, B., Wang, N., Chen, T., Li, M.: Empirical evaluation of rectified activations in convolutional network (2015). arXiv:1505.00853

23. Zhang, H., Yushkevich, P.A., Alexander, D.C., Gee, J.C.: Deformable registration of diffusion tensor MR images with explicit orientation optimization. Med. Image Anal. **10**(5), 764–785 (2006). The Eighth International Conference on Medical Imaging and Computer Assisted Intervention - MICCAI 2005

Automated Multi-class Fetal Cardiac Vessel Segmentation in Aortic Arch Anomalies Using T2-Weighted 3D Fetal MRI

Paula Ramirez Gilliland[✉], Alena Uus, Milou P. M. van Poppel,
Irina Grigorescu, Johannes K. Steinweg, David F. A. Lloyd,
Kuberan Pushparajah, Andrew P. King, and Maria Deprez

School of Biomedical Engineering and Imaging Sciences, King's College London,
London, UK
paula.ramirez_gilliland@kcl.ac.uk

Abstract. Congenital heart disease (CHD) encompasses a range of cardiac malformations present from birth, representing the leading congenital diagnosis. 3D volumetric reconstructions of T2w black blood fetal MRI provide optimal vessel visualisation, supporting prenatal CHD diagnosis, a key step for optimal patient management. We present a framework for automated multi-class fetal vessel segmentation in the setting where binary manual labels of the vessels region of interest (ROI) are available for training, as well as a multi-class labelled atlas.

We combine deep learning label propagation from multi-class labelled condition-specific atlases with 3D Attention U-Net segmentation to achieve the desired multi-class output. We train a single network to segment 12 fetal cardiac vessels for three distinct aortic arch anomalies (double aortic arch, right aortic arch, and suspected coarctation of the aorta). Our segmentation network is trained by combination of a multi-class loss, which uses the propagated multi-class labels; and a binary loss which uses binary labels generated by expert clinicians.

Our proposed method outperforms label propagation in accuracy of vessel segmentation, while succeeding in segmenting the anomaly area of all three CHD diagnoses included, achieving a 100% vessel detection rate.

Keywords: Automated Segmentation · Congenital Heart Disease · Fetal Cardiac MRI · Label Propagation · Atlas-based segmentation

1 Introduction

Congenital heart disease (CHD) refers to a range of cardiac defects present from birth, constituting the leading mortality cause related to congenital defects [9].

Fetal cardiac MR (CMR) has the potential of becoming widespread for prenatal CHD diagnosis as an adjunct to echocardiography [8]. State-of-the-art

R. Licandro et al. (Eds.): PIPPI 2022, LNCS 13575, pp. 82–93, 2022.
https://doi.org/10.1007/978-3-031-17117-8_8

reconstruction algorithms [19] address fetal CMR motion challenges, allowing to generate high quality 3D reconstructions, with T2w black blood MRI being particularly favourable for vascular assessments [8].

Routine clinical fetal cardiac assessments involve the time-consuming task of manual region of interest (ROI) segmentation, for visualisation and reporting purposes. This is generally a binary mask, as multi-class labels are too laborious to produce in clinical practice. Multi-class vessel information is desirable, enabling to efficiently localise the anomaly area. We propose to address this need via deep learning, being the method of choice for state-of-the-art segmentation performance.

Training a CNN for segmentation typically requires a large number of manually labelled examples. However, producing a large number of multi-class labellings of 3D fetal CMR images is unfeasible in this setting. Therefore, we propose a novel deep learning framework, combining label propagation from a multi-class condition-specific atlas, with manual binary vascular ROI segmentations (see Fig. 1) for training a 3D Attention U-Net [10] to predict high quality multi-class segmentations.

We propagate the desired multi-class protocol from the pertinent fetal cardiac atlas (Fig. 1 left), and achieve high accuracy in individual images by virtue of the manual binary vessels ROI labels (Fig. 1 right). Our fully automated multi-class segmentation technique will aid fetal cardiac vessel visualisation for prenatal diagnostic reporting purposes, providing the basis for automated vessel biometry and detection.

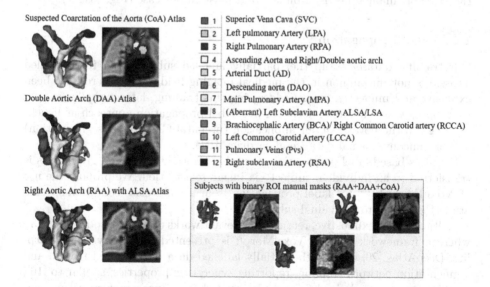

Fig. 1. Left: 3D T2w MRI aortic arch anomaly atlases with multi-class vessel segmentations. Right: 3D reconstructed images with binary manual labels.

1.1   Deep Learning Segmentation

U-Net [14] architectures are widely used for medical image segmentation, and have been employed for fetal brain and thorax MRI segmentation [15,17].

There have been many applications of deep learning for adult CMR segmentation in CHD [1]. For instance, Yu et al. [21] achieved promising results for whole heart and great vessel segmentation by employing a deeply supervised 3D fractal network. In [11], an iterative segmentation method based on a recurrent neural network is proposed, aiming to mitigate limited training data. Rezaei et al. present a framework comprising a three-stage cascade of conditional GANs for whole heart and great vessel segmentation in CHD [13].

We do not explore these approaches as our dataset is not comparable, due to anatomical and size differences between adult and fetal subjects, and distinct acquisition and reconstruction protocols.

Attention U-Net. Attention U-Net [10] incorporates an attention gate into a standard U-Net architecture, filtering the skip connection features. This allows the network to focus on important and diverse structures, eliminating redundant regions. We use this network architecture as our target vessels present large variations regarding shape and location, further emphasised by the three diagnoses used. We further motivate our network choice by qualitatively comparing performance against a standard U-Net architecture (Sect. 3.1).

However, Attention U-Net for segmentation is restricted to the protocol of the available manual labels, a binary ROI mask in our case (Fig. 1 right).

1.2   Label Propagation

Our training dataset setup (i.e. partially labelled subjects and fully-labelled atlases) is not uncommon in the medical imaging field. While there have been extensive and innovative works addressing this training dataset challenge [12], we propose to use a simple deep learning label propagation approach as benchmark, given the novelty of our application (prenatal CHD vessel segmentation) and our unconventional data (fetal cardiac MRI).

In atlas-based label propagation, the label information from a given atlas is transferred to an individual subject via image registration. We propose the use of **VoxelMorph** [2] for label propagation from a multi-class condition-specific atlas (Fig. 1 left) to individual subjects.

Although not exhaustive, recent and relevant works to our method include [3], where a framework akin to VoxelMorph is presented for binary mask warping. DeepAtlas [20] deals with partially labelled data by joint registration and segmentation network training, reporting synergistic properties, similar to [16], where a population-derived atlas is constructed in the process. Generating synthetic labelled data using VoxelMorph has been proposed to ameliorate misregistration artefacts [23]. These strategies therefore offer many avenues for future refinement of our work, given the framework similarity (VoxelMorph).

Label propagation allows to transfer any desired segmentation protocol from the atlas to each subject image, but is limited by registration quality. We address this challenge by including Attention U-Net for segmentation refinement.

1.3   Contribution

We present an automated multi-class fetal cardiac segmentation approach which only requires manual binary ROI masks (Fig. 1 right) and a multi-class atlas for training, and thus is adaptable to clinical environments. Our framework combines deep learning label propagation of any desired multi-class protocol with highly accurate Attention U-Net segmentation. We build on prior research on fetal cardiac atlas development and atlas-guided segmentation [18] to present the first fully automated, fully deep learning approach for multi-class fetal CMR vessel segmentation, addressing aortic arch anomalies. We target subjects with Double Aortic Arch (DAA), Right Aortic Arch (RAA) with Aberrant Left Subclavian Artery (ALSA), and suspected Coarctation of the Aorta (CoA).

2   Methods

2.1   Data Specifications

Our dataset consists of 189 fetal subjects with suspected coarctation of the aorta (CoA, N = 90), Right Aortic Arch (RAA) with ALSA (N = 70) and Double Aortic Arch (DAA, N = 29), 31.4 ± 1.5 weeks mean GA. The datasets were acquired at Evelina London Children's Hospital using a 1.5 T Tesla Ingenia MRI system, T2-weighted SSFSE sequence (RT = 20,000 ms, ET = 50 ms, FA = $90°$, voxel size = 1.25×1.25 mm, slice thickness = 2.5 mm and slice overlap = 1.25 mm). All research participants provided written informed consent. The raw datasets comprised 6–12 multi-slice 2D stacks, covering the fetal thorax in three orthogonal planes.

We used images reconstructed both with Slice-to-Volume Registration (SVR, lower quality, N = 139) [6,7], and with Deformable SVR [19] (DSVR, higher quality, N = 50) to 0.75 mm isotropic resolution, to ensure a varied dataset.

The majority of these subjects (N = 181) were manually segmented by trained clinicians using ITK-SNAP [22], encompassing the main cardiac vessels region (binary manual label). For the remaining unsegmented subjects (N = 15) we exclusively use propagated atlas labels for network training (Sect. 2.2).

In order to achieve our multi-class output, we employ three fully-labelled atlases[1] (see Fig. 1), one per condition (RAA, DAA and CoA). These include 12 manually segmented vascular regions for RAA and DAA, and 11 for CoA cases.

We crop all data to the cardiac vessels region, and split the subjects into a training set ($N_{CoA} = 71$, $N_{RAA} = 55$, $N_{DAA} = 21$), validation set ($N_{CoA} = 3$, $N_{RAA} = 3$, $N_{DAA} = 3$), and testing set ($N_{CoA} = 16$, $N_{RAA} = 12$, $N_{DAA} = 5$). We normalise and rescale the intensity between 0 and 1, and use a weighted random sampler to ensure equal probabilistic sampling from each diagnosis.

---

[1] https://gin.g-node.org/SVRTK/.

2.2   Deep Learning Segmentation Framework

Our framework consists of Attention U-Net [10] trained using a combination of manual binary labels and multi-class labels, propagated from an atlas using deep learning registration (VoxelMorph [2], Sect. 2.3). The input of the segmentation network is an MRI image and output is a multi-class segmentation.

The proposed segmentation network is trained using two losses: (1) a multi-class loss between the propagated labels and U-Net predictions; (2) a binary loss between the predicted multi-class labels joined into a binary segmentation and manual binary labels (Sect. 2.4). We exclusively employ the multi-class loss for the subset of subjects with no binary manual labels. Our training strategy, *U-Net LP + man*, is illustrated in Fig. 2.

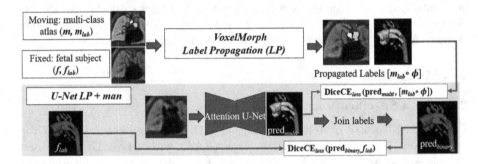

Fig. 2. Our proposed framework (*U-Net LP + man*) is trained by combination of a multi-class loss with the propagated labels, and a binary loss with the manual binary ROI masks. Three atlases are used (CoA, RAA, DAA), subject to case diagnosis.

2.3   Label Propagation

We use VoxelMorph [2] for label propagation. We define our atlases as the moving images (m), and the subject images as fixed images (f). We use the prior knowledge of condition diagnosis to select the pertinent atlas to each case.

Label Propagation Loss Functions: We use Local Normalised Cross Correlation loss (LNCC$_{loss}$) [2] as a **similarity loss** function ($\mathcal{L}_{sim}$), and Dice Loss between propagated joined atlas labels and binary manual masks as an **auxiliary segmentation loss** function ($\mathcal{L}_{seg}$). We include a regularisation penalty for the displacement field as a bending energy **BE loss** ($\mathcal{L}_{BE}$), as described in [4]. The **total registration loss** $\mathcal{L}_{reg}$ may be expressed as

$$\mathcal{L}_{reg} = \mathcal{L}_{sim}(f, m \cdot \phi) + \lambda_1 \mathcal{L}_{BE}(\phi) + \lambda_2 \mathcal{L}_{seg}, \qquad (1)$$

where λ_1 and λ_2 are loss weights.

Registration Network Implementation Details: We employ a U-Net based encoder-decoder architecture with skip connections. Output channels are 16, 32, 32, 64 for the encoder (blocks of 3D strided convolutions with leaky ReLU activations); and 32, 32, 32 for the decoder (blocks of strided transpose 3D convolutions and leaky ReLU activations), followed by two convolutional blocks. This is depicted in Fig. 3.

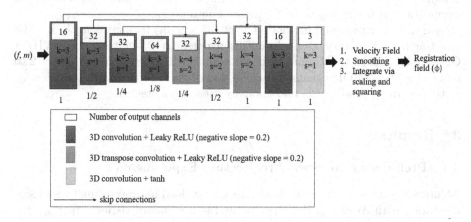

Fig. 3. CNN architecture used for registration. The numbers under each convolution representation indicate the volume spatial resolution relative to the input volume. k = kernel size, s = stride.

We train a single CNN on all diagnoses, appropriately pairing each subject to its corresponding atlas. We train VoxelMorph registration network until convergence (28,430 iterations, NVIDIA GeForce RTX 3090 GPU), using a linearly decaying learning rate initialised at 5×10^{-4}, and an Adam optimiser (default β parameters, weight decay of 1×10^{-5}). We implement the LNCC_{loss} using $n = 9$, $\lambda_1 = 0.2$, and $\lambda_2 = 1$ and set the standard deviation of the velocity field smoothing kernel to 2. We affinely register all subject images to the atlas prior to training. We use Project MONAI spatial and intensity data augmentation[2]

2.4 Attention U-Net Segmentation

Segmentation Loss Function: We use the **soft dice and cross entropy loss** [5] (DiceCE_{loss}) for all our segmentation experiments. Our proposed framework *U-Net LP + man* is trained using a combined loss

$$\mathcal{L}_{seg} = \text{DiceCE}_{loss}(\text{pred}_{multi}, [m_{\text{lab}} \cdot \phi]) + \lambda_3 \text{DiceCE}_{loss}(\text{pred}_{joined}, f_{lab}) \quad (2)$$

where pred_{multi} are the multi-class Attention U-Net predictions, pred_{joined} are binary label predictions (multi-class output labels joined together), $[m_{\text{lab}} \cdot \phi]$ are the propagated atlas labels, f_{lab} are the manual binary labels and λ_3 is the binary loss weight. The proposed losses are schematically presented in Fig. 2.

---

[2] https://github.com/Project-MONAI/MONAI/.

Segmentation Network Implementation Details: We use a 3D Attention U-Net [10] (Project MONAI implementatio (see Footnote 2)) for automated segmentation, with five encoder-decoder blocks (output channels 32, 64, 128, 256 and 512), convolution and upsampling kernel size of 3, ReLU activation, dropout ratio of 0.5, batch normalisation, and a batch size of 12. We employ an AdamW optimiser with linearly decaying learning rate, initialised at 1×10^{-3}, default β parameters and weight decay $= 1 \times 10^{-5}$. We use intensity and spatial augmentations from Project MONAI (see Footnote 2)].

We train our proposed method (*U-Net LP + man*) by increasing λ_3 by 0.05 (starting from 0.0) every 50 epochs until convergence (12,689 iterations, NVIDIA GeForce RTX 3090 GPU), and train for a further 274 iterations with $\lambda_3 = 2$ to refine the vessels ROI segmentation. We do not train further with a higher λ_3, as this degrades small vessel and anomaly area segmentation.

3   Results

3.1   Preliminary Network Architecture Experiments

Ablation experiments on network architecture yielded improved small vessel segmentation with Attention U-Net, compared to a standard U-Net [14] (Fig. 4).

GT   Standard U-Net   Attention U-Net

Fig. 4. Improved small vessel segmentation in a RAA subject (circle) when using Attention U-Net as opposed to a standard U-Net (same architecture). GT is ground truth.

3.2   Test Set and Experiments

We manually generated multi-class ground truth (GT) labels for our test set (N = 33) via ITK-SNAP [22]. We compute multi-class Dice scores and average distance scores for each vessel, presented alongside the average of the 95th percentile of the Hausdorff Distance (HD95) across all class scores (Table 1).

Training Experiments: We compare our proposed approach (*U-Net LP + man*) with binary manual label loss and propagated atlas label loss (Eq. 2) to VoxelMorph label propagation (*LP*), multi-class Attention U-Net trained exclusively on propagated labels (*U-Net LP*), and baseline binary Attention

U-Net trained exclusively on manual segmentations (**U-Net man**). We offer
visual assessments and vessel detection rates to compare our binary network to
our multi-class approaches.

3.3 Quantitative Results

Table 1. Mean multi-class test set Dice scores, average surface distance (ASD) scores
(standard deviation), and averaged HD95 scores over all vessels, compared to manually
generated multi-class GT.

	LP		U-Net LP		U-Net LP + man	
Vessel	Dice	ASD	Dice	ASD	Dice	ASD
SVC	0.61 (0.19)	1.70 (1.30)	0.66 (0.09)	1.41 (0.58)	**0.74 (0.08)**	**1.08 (0.47)**
LPA	0.46 (0.16)	3.63 (2.13)	0.49 (0.11)	3.21 (1.74)	**0.57 (0.10)**	**2.54 (1.49)**
RPA	0.42 (0.14)	4.40 (2.58)	0.45 (0.10)	4.14 (2.09)	**0.52 (0.09)**	**3.35 (1.76)**
Aorta	0.53 (0.13)	1.57 (0.69)	0.57 (0.08)	1.45 (0.29)	**0.72 (0.05)**	**0.98 (0.13)**
AD	0.70 (0.18)	1.03 (0.90)	0.74 (0.09)	0.82 (0.21)	**0.78 (0.09)**	**0.71 (0.19)**
DAO	0.76 (0.09)	0.97 (0.43)	0.79 (0.05)	0.89 (0.21)	**0.85 (0.04)**	**0.67 (0.31)**
MPA	0.68 (0.09)	1.33 (0.43)	0.69 (0.05)	1.36 (0.28)	**0.80 (0.04)**	**0.92 (0.20)**
Head and neck vess.	0.32 (0.20)	2.40 (1.96)	0.34 (0.18)	2.02 (1.30)	**0.36 (0.18)**	**1.90 (1.22)**
Pvs	0.26 (0.12)	2.32 (1.21)	0.29 (0.12)	2.17 (0.91)	**0.37 (0.12)**	**1.81 (0.74)**
Averaged vessel HD95	7.30 (5.02)		6.86 (4.96)		**6.09 (4.51)**	

In Table 1 we quantitatively compare our three multi-label segmentation
approaches (Sect. 3.2). Our results demonstrate that combining propagated
multi-class labels and manual binary labels during training leads to improved segmentation performance, as opposed to exclusively employing propagated labels.
Our proposed framework (*U-Net LP + man*) achieves the highest scores for all
individual vessels, for all metrics compared (dice scores, ASD, HD95). The head
and neck vessels (LSA/ALSA, BCA/RCCA, LCCA and RSA) present lower Dice
scores due to their small size (see Fig. 1).

Discussing the performance of our networks in a clinical context is challenging, given that, due to the novelty of our dataset, the field standards have yet
to be defined. We therefore present our results as an initial benchmark.

A challenge and limitation of our approach (particularly regarding evaluation) lies in the inherent differences between manually segmented labels and
multi-class atlases. The latter comprises an idealised MRI representation of the
conditions investigated, where all vessels are fully visible. This is not always the
case in our training data, where certain subjects present lower visibility in specific anatomical locations (due to low image quality, low contrast, or anatomical
variability), rendering segmentation of small vessels highly challenging. For this
reason, some of our manually segmented vessels, which we consider to be GT, are
shorter in length compared to the atlas (i.e. present partially segmented vessels).
The consistency of our network predictions regarding vessel length (due to our

use of propagated labels during training) may decrease the performance metrics for these cases, despite anatomical correctness.

We attempt to circumvent this evaluation limitation by offering a qualitative visual assessment, in addition to having our predictions inspected by a trained clinician.

3.4 Visual Inspection

Our predictions were inspected by a trained clinician, reporting overall optimal results, with higher anatomically correctness from our full multi-class framework predictions (*U-Net LP+man*) compared to our binary predictions (*U-Net man*). Discrepancies were observed in the pulmonary veins region (which is less relevant to the conditions investigated). However these vessels remain challenging to discern in our data, given the homogeneously contrasted surroundings.

Our proposed framework (*U-Net LP+man*) outperforms *U-Net man* in small vessel detection and anomaly area segmentation (see Table 2). This is particularly relevant for subjects with DAA, where our full framework fully segments the anomaly area in all test set cases, while the network trained just on binary masks (*U-Net man*) only segmented one case correctly. Nevertheless our DAA test set sample is too small to extract substantial conclusions (N = 5).

Table 2. Test set detection rates on head and neck vessels and anomaly area for the three conditions investigated (RAA, DAA, suspected CoA).

Anatomical location	*U-Net man*	*U-Net LP*	*U-Net LP + man*
Aorta (CoA)	93.8%	100%	100%
Double Arch (DAA)	20%	100%	100%
Right Arch (RAA)	100%	100%	100%
Head and neck vessels (CoA)	81.3%	100%	100%
Head and neck vessels (RAA)	66.7%	100%	100%
Head and neck vessels (DAA)	60%	100%	100%

The head and neck vessels are always detected with *U-Net LP+man*, while *U-Net man* misses at least one small vessel in 10 out of 33 test set subjects (see Table 2). Thus, targeting vessels individually enhances small vessel detection. This is particularly relevant to subjects with DAA and RAA, where the suboptimal performance of *U-Net man* may be due to the fact that these conditions present an additional head and neck vessel (four) compared to cases with suspected coarctation of the aorta (three). Having a multi-class approach enables the network to learn the class and location of each vessel, allowing for greater anatomically sound predictions.

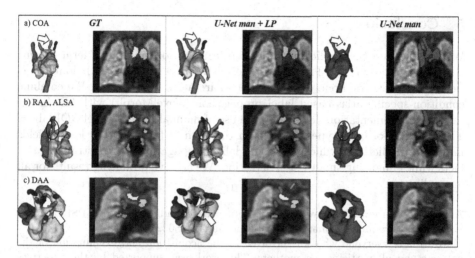

Fig. 5. Test set network prediction examples for CoA, RAA and DAA, showcasing improved small vessel detection and anomaly area segmentation with our full framework.

Figure 5 depicts examples where *U-Net LP + man* outperforms *U-Net man*. For the CoA case (Fig. 5a), LCCA remains unsegmented in *U-Net man*, contrary to our full framework. In the RAA example (Fig. 5b), RCCA is fused to SVC in the binary approach (*U-Net man*), while our multi-class approach minimises these biologically unfeasible predictions. Lastly *U-Net man* fully misses the double arch (a key DAA biomarker) in Fig. 5c, contrasting with *U-Net man + LP*.

4   Discussion

Our proposed framework (*U-Net LP+man*) combines training using propagated multi-class labels and manual binary labels, resulting in automated multi-class segmentation with enhanced performance and small vessel segmentation. We overcome misregistration artefacts from the propagated labels by utilising manually segmented vessels ROI masks. Our tunable binary loss weight allows to explore the optimal trade-off between losses, resulting in optimal segmentation accuracy and 100% small vessel detection. We achieve correct anomaly area segmentation for DAA, RAA and suspected CoA cases from a single network.

Although we employ simple and well established methods, our training strategy is applicable to analogous tasks with a similar dataset setup. For instance, cases with low image quality may benefit from incorporating prior shape, contextual and textural knowledge in the form of an atlas. Likewise, for multi-organ segmentation, clinical datasets often include images where only a certain organ of interest is segmented. Utilising additional available atlas information could aid in attaining the desired output.

5   Conclusion

We demonstrate the applicability of deep learning for multi-class fetal cardiac vessel segmentation from T2w 3D MRI reconstructions for cases with double aortic arch, right aortic arch, and suspected coarctation of the aorta. We combine condition-specific atlas-based label propagation (VoxelMorph) with 3D Attention U-Net segmentation, leveraging the use of manual binary vessel ROI labels. The inclusion of both types of labels in the form of two weighted losses yields improved predictions, which overcome label propagation misregistration artefacts while enhancing small vessel detection. We achieve promising results for all anomalies.

Acknowledgements. We would like to acknowledge funding from the EPSRC Centre for Doctoral Training in Smart Medical Imaging (EP/S022104/1).

We thank everyone who was involved in the acquisition and examination of the datasets and all participating mothers. This work was supported by the Rosetrees Trust [A2725], the Wellcome/EPSRC Centre for Medical Engineering at King's College London [WT 203148/Z/16/Z], the Wellcome Trust and EPSRC IEH award [102431] for the iFIND project, the NIHR Clinical Research Facility (CRF) at Guy's and St Thomas' and by the National Institute for Health Research Biomedical Research Centre based at Guy's and St Thomas' NHS Foundation Trust and King's College London. The views expressed are those of the authors and not necessarily those of the NHS, the NIHR or the Department of Health.

References

1. Arafati, A., et al.: Artificial intelligence in pediatric and adult congenital cardiac MRI: an unmet clinical need. Cardiovasc. Diagn. Ther. **9**(Suppl 2), S310 (2019)
2. Balakrishnan, G., Zhao, A., Sabuncu, M.R., Guttag, J., Dalca, A.V.: VoxelMorph: a learning framework for deformable medical image registration. IEEE Trans. Med. Imaging **38**(8), 1788–1800 (2019)
3. Dinsdale, N.K., Jenkinson, M., Namburete, A.I.L.: Spatial warping network for 3D segmentation of the hippocampus in MR images. In: Shen, D., et al. (eds.) MICCAI 2019. LNCS, vol. 11766, pp. 284–291. Springer, Cham (2019). https://doi.org/10.1007/978-3-030-32248-9_32
4. Grigorescu, I., et al.: Diffusion tensor driven image registration: a deep learning approach. In: Špiclin, Ž, McClelland, J., Kybic, J., Goksel, O. (eds.) WBIR 2020. LNCS, vol. 12120, pp. 131–140. Springer, Cham (2020). https://doi.org/10.1007/978-3-030-50120-4_13
5. Hatamizadeh, A., et al.: UNETR: transformers for 3D medical image segmentation. In: Proceedings of the IEEE/CVF Winter Conference on Applications of Computer Vision, pp. 574–584 (2022)
6. Kainz, B., et al.: Fast volume reconstruction from motion corrupted stacks of 2D slices. IEEE Trans. Med. Imaging **34**(9), 1901–1913 (2015)
7. Kuklisova-Murgasova, M., Quaghebeur, G., Rutherford, M.A., Hajnal, J.V., Schnabel, J.A.: Reconstruction of fetal brain MRI with intensity matching and complete outlier removal. Med. Image Anal. **16**(8), 1550–1564 (2012)

8. Lloyd, D.F., et al.: Three-dimensional visualisation of the fetal heart using prenatal MRI with motion-corrected slice-volume registration: a prospective, single-centre cohort study. The Lancet **393**(10181), 1619–1627 (2019)

9. Mendis, S., Puska, P., Norrving, B., Organization, W.H., et al.: Global Atlas on Cardiovascular Disease Prevention and Control. World Health Organization (2011)

10. Oktay, O., et al.: Attention U-Net: learning where to look for the pancreas. arXiv preprint arXiv:1804.03999 (2018)

11. Pace, D.F., et al.: Iterative segmentation from limited training data: applications to congenital heart disease. In: Stoyanov, D., et al. (eds.) DLMIA/ML-CDS -2018. LNCS, vol. 11045, pp. 334–342. Springer, Cham (2018). https://doi.org/10.1007/978-3-030-00889-5_38

12. Peng, J., Wang, Y.: Medical image segmentation with limited supervision: a review of deep network models. IEEE Access **9**, 36827–36851 (2021)

13. Rezaei, M., Yang, H., Meinel, C.: Whole heart and great vessel segmentation with context-aware of generative adversarial networks. In: Maier, A., Deserno, T., Handels, H., Maier-Hein, K., Palm, C., Tolxdorff, T. (eds.) Bildverarbeitung für die Medizin 2018. I, pp. 353–358. Springer, Heidelberg (2018). https://doi.org/10.1007/978-3-662-56537-7_89

14. Ronneberger, O., Fischer, P., Brox, T.: U-Net: convolutional networks for biomedical image segmentation. In: Navab, N., Hornegger, J., Wells, W.M., Frangi, A.F. (eds.) MICCAI 2015. LNCS, vol. 9351, pp. 234–241. Springer, Cham (2015). https://doi.org/10.1007/978-3-319-24574-4_28

15. Salehi, S.S.M., et al.: Real-time automatic fetal brain extraction in fetal MRI by deep learning. In: 2018 IEEE 15th International Symposium on Biomedical Imaging (ISBI 2018), pp. 720–724. IEEE (2018)

16. Sinclair, M., et al.: Atlas-ISTN: joint segmentation, registration and atlas construction with image-and-spatial transformer networks. Med. Image Anal. **78**, 102383 (2022)

17. Uus, A., et al.: 3D UNet with GAN discriminator for robust localisation of the fetal brain and trunk in MRI with partial coverage of the fetal body. BioRxiv (2021)

18. Uus, A., et al.: 3D MRI atlases of congenital aortic arch anomalies and normal fetal heart: application to automated multi-label segmentation. BioRxiv (2022)

19. Uus, A., et al.: Deformable slice-to-volume registration for motion correction of fetal body and placenta MRI. IEEE Trans. Med. Imaging **39**(9), 2750–2759 (2020)

20. Xu, Z., Niethammer, M.: DeepAtlas: joint semi-supervised learning of image registration and segmentation. In: Shen, D., et al. (eds.) MICCAI 2019. LNCS, vol. 11765, pp. 420–429. Springer, Cham (2019). https://doi.org/10.1007/978-3-030-32245-8_47

21. Yu, L., Yang, X., Qin, J., Heng, P.-A.: 3D FractalNet: dense volumetric segmentation for cardiovascular MRI volumes. In: Zuluaga, M.A., Bhatia, K., Kainz, B., Moghari, M.H., Pace, D.F. (eds.) RAMBO/HVSMR -2016. LNCS, vol. 10129, pp. 103–110. Springer, Cham (2017). https://doi.org/10.1007/978-3-319-52280-7_10

22. Yushkevich, P.A., et al.: User-guided 3D active contour segmentation of anatomical structures: significantly improved efficiency and reliability. Neuroimage **31**(3), 1116–1128 (2006)

23. Zhao, A., Balakrishnan, G., Durand, F., Guttag, J.V., Dalca, A.V.: Data augmentation using learned transformations for one-shot medical image segmentation. In: Proceedings of the IEEE/CVF Conference on Computer Vision and Pattern Recognition, pp. 8543–8553 (2019)

Segmentation of Periventricular White Matter in Neonatal Brain MRI: Analysis of Brain Maturation in Term and Preterm Cohorts

Alena U. Uus[1]([✉]), Mohammad-Usamah Ayub[1], Abi Gartner[2],
Vanessa Kyriakopoulou[2], Maximilian Pietsch[2], Irina Grigorescu[1],
Daan Christiaens[1,3], Jana Hutter[1], Lucilio Cordero Grande[2,4], Anthony Price[2],
Dafnis Batalle[2,5], Serena Counsell[2], Joseph V. Hajnal[1,2], A. David Edwards[2],
Mary A. Rutherford[2], and Maria Deprez[1]

[1] Biomedical Engineering Department, School of Imaging Sciences and Biomedical
Engineering, King's College London, St. Thomas' Hospital, London, UK
Alena.Uus@kcl.ac.uk
[2] Centre for the Developing Brain, School Biomedical Engineering and Imaging
Sciences, King's College London, St Thomas' Hospital, London, UK
[3] Department of Electrical Engineering, ESAT-PSI, KU Leuven, Leuven, Belgium
[4] Department of Forensic and Neurodevelopmental Science, Institute of Psychiatry,
Psychology and Neuroscience, King's College London, London, UK
[5] Biomedical Image Technologies, ETSI Telecomunicacion, Universidad Politécnica
de Madrid and CIBER-BBN, Madrid, Spain

Abstract. MRI is conventionally employed in neonatal brain diagnosis
and research studies. However, the traditional segmentation protocols
omit differentiation between heterogeneous white matter (WM) tissue
zones that rapidly evolve and change during the early brain development. There is a reported correlations of characteristics of the transient WM compartments (including periventricular regions, subplate,
etc.) with brain maturation [23,26] and neurodevelopment scores [22].
However, there are no currently available standards for parcellation of
these regions in MRI scans. Therefore, in this work, we propose the first
deep learning solution for automated 3D segmentation of periventricular
WM (PWM) regions that would be the first step towards tissue-specific
WM analysis. The implemented segmentation method based on UNETR
[13] was then used for assessment of the differences between term and
preterm cohorts (200 subjects) from the developing Human Connectome
Project (dHCP) (dHCP) project [1] in terms of the ROI-specific volumetry and microstructural diffusion MRI indices.

Keywords: Neonatal brain MRI · Periventricular white matter ·
Brain maturation · Automated segmentation

© The Author(s), under exclusive license to Springer Nature Switzerland AG 2022
R. Licandro et al. (Eds.): PIPPI 2022, LNCS 13575, pp. 94–104, 2022.
https://doi.org/10.1007/978-3-031-17117-8_9

1   Introduction

Segmentation of T2w structural neonatal brain MRI is conventionally employed in neurodevelopment research studies [9] and there are many existing automated pipelines. These solutions are based on either classical (e.g., label propagation, intensity classification) [6,18,21,26] or deep neural network [10,12] methods. In the majority of these methods, the white matter (WM) is classified as a single tissue component [6,10,18] or subdivided into standard anatomical regions [5,12,21,24] that follow the adult brain parcellation protocols (e.g., temporal lobe, corpus callosum, etc.). However, during the neonatal brain development the WM tissue is highly heterogeneous and constantly evolving due to the different rates of tract maturation and myelination. The example in Fig. 1 shows the regional difference of T2 MRI signal intensities in WM at different ages: 38 to 44 weeks post-menstrual age (PMA). The hyperintense T2 signal regions in WM reportedly correspond the higher water content [11] and are also sometimes referred to as diffuse excessive high signal intensity (DEHSI) ROIs [22] or transient WM [15,23]. These tissue types are transient by nature and eventually are expected to disappear by changing properties and evolving into mature WM tissue. Recently, [23] formalised a new neonatal brain maturation MRI scoring protocol based on the appearance of WM transient compartments including periventricular crossroads, von Monakow WM segments, subplate and germinal matrix. The higher proportion of transient WM are correlated with lower degree of brain maturation. However, apart from the works on segmentation of DEHSI [20,22] or high rate change WM regions [26] that are related to transient WM structures, there has been no reported works on automation of parcellation of specific types of WM tissue defined in [23]. These transient WM ROIs are characterised by the prolonged coexistence in preterm brain [16,23] while periventricular WM is vulnerable to injury [17]. There is also no formalised reference parcellation protocol for transient WM tissue, which is required for development of new automated methods or even simple manual segmentation for quantitative studies.

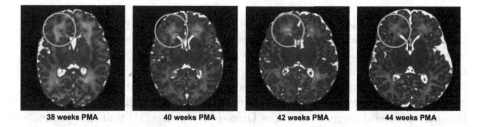

Fig. 1. Examples of WM tissue heterogeneity in transient compartments visible on T2w neonatal brain MRI at different PMA (the datasets are from dHCP project [1]).

Contributions: In this work, we propose the first deep learning based pipeline for automated segmentation of periventricular white matter (PWM) in neonatal

T2w MRI scans. This extends the already existing solutions [12] for volumetry-based analysis of brain development. The feasibility of the segmentation pipeline is assessed with respect to analysis of the difference between term and preterm cohorts for 200 neonatal subjects from the dHCP project. The PWM segmentations from the proposed pipeline were used for both volumetry and calculation ROI-average microstructural diffusion tensor imaging (DTI) indices.

2   Methods

2.1   Cohort, Datasets and Preprocessing

The MRI datasets used in this study were acquired as a part of the dHCP project [1] available via the public release. The selected cohort includes 150 term (37–44 weeks gestational age (GA) at birth) and 50 preterm ($\leq$32 weeks GA at birth) neonates scanned between 38 and 44 weeks PMA (Fig. 2). The selection criteria was the absence of major anomalies and good image quality.

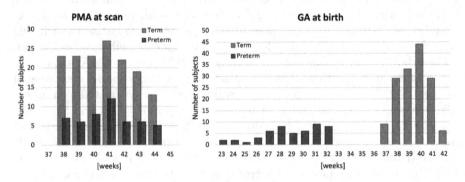

Fig. 2. PMA at scan and GA at birth of the investigated neonatal MRI datasets from the dHCP project: term and preterm cohorts.

Each dataset includes diffusion and structural T2w MRI volumes. The acquisitions were performed on a 3T Philips scanner with a 32-channel neonatal head coil and transportation system [14]. The structural T2w volumes were acquired using a TSE sequence with TR = 12 s, TE = 156 ms. The isotropic T2w volumes were reconstructed to 0.5 mm resolution using a combination of motion correction [8] and super-resolution reconstruction [19]. All volumes were N4 bias corrected and normalised in the Draw-EM pipeline [21] that also produced brain tissue parcellation maps. The multi-shell high angular resolution dMRI volumes were acquired with four phase-encode directions on four shells (b-values: 0, 400, 1000 and 2600 s/mm^2) with TE = 90 ms, TR = 3800 ms Hutter2018 with 1.5 × 1.5 × 3 mm resolution and 1.5 mm slice overlap and reconstructed to 1.5 mm isotropic resolution using the SHARD pipeline [7] that also includes slice-wise motion correction, distortion correction, exclusion of corrupted slices and essential preprocessing. The extraction of fractional anisotropy (FA) and mean diffusivity (MD) DTI metrics was performed in MRtrix3 [25] toolbox. The structural to dMRI volumes were co-aligned using T2 to MD affine registration in MRtrix3.

2.2 Parcellation Map of Periventricular WM ROIs in the Atlas Space

In order to provide the basis for the automated segmentation pipeline, we defined the first parcellation map of PWM in the MRI atlas space based on the guidance from the clinical MRI studies [15,23]. We used the T2w channel of the 4D neonatal MRI atlas from [26] (36 weeks PMA time-point, 0.5 mm isotropic resolution) as the reference space for segmentation of five periventricular WM regions. The atlas includes the high rate change WM parcellation map, which we subdivided and refined based on the definition of the PWM ROIs (also referred to as "periventricular crossroads") described and illustrated in [15,23]. Refinement was performed manually in ITK-SNAP [2] based on T2 signal intensity boundaries by a researcher with experience in neonatal MRI. The PWM regions were the segmented and named based on the definitions in [23]. This was followed by separation into left and right resulting in ten label ROIs.

2.3 Automated Segmentation of Periventricular WM ROIs

To our knowledge, there has been no reported works on automated segmentation of PWM in neonatal brain MRI. The only relevant methods that addressed the tissue-specific delineation of WM were proposed for segmentation of DEHSI [20,22] and high rate change [26] WM regions. These solutions are based on classical intensity thresholding and atlas label propagation, which tend to be prone to errors and sensitive to image quality and preprocessing. This limits their large scale application. As an alternative, we propose to use deep learning for 3D segmentation of multiple PWM regions [23] based on the protocol defined in Sect. 2.2 and [23]. The proposed solution is summarised in Fig. 3.

Deep Learning Model for Automated PWM Segmentation: In this work, we used the recently proposed vision transformer based deep neural network segmentation technique (UNETR) [13], as it has shown to perform well for 3D multi-label segmentation. The proposed segmentation pipeline was implemented in MONAI Pytorch-based framework [4]. We selected the default UNETR configuration with combined Dice and cross entropy Loss, AdamW optimiser, $160 \times 160 \times 160$ input size and six output channels (3 left and right PWM regions). For this segmentation network, we selected only the three largest PWM ROIs defined in the atlas space because of the significantly smaller size and lower visibility of the other two regions [23].

Generations of Labels for Training: In this case, there were no available manual parcellations of PWM in subject T2w volumes for training due to the time-consuming segmentation of these large regions as well as the difficulty in delineation of not well defined tissue boundaries. Therefore, we created the labels for

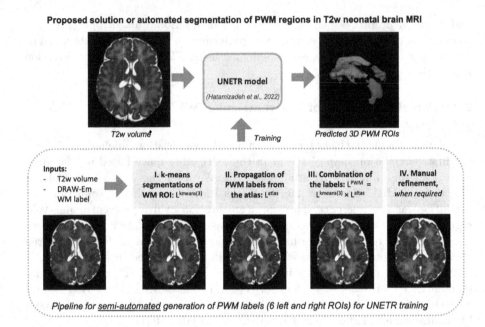

Fig. 3. Proposed solution for automated segmentation of PWM in T2w neonatal brain MRI based on UNETR [13] and semi-automated generation of the labels for training.

training of the UNETR network using a semi-automated approach based on the combination of classical methods (see Fig. 3) and manual refinement. At first, kmeans segmentation (from MIRTK toolbox [3]) is used for parcellation of the T2w image within the WM ROI (from the DRAW-EM labels) into 3 clusters. We select only the cluster with the highest intensity. Next, we run propagation of the PWM labels (Sect. 2.2) based on subject-atlas multi-channel registration [26] in MRtrix3 [25]. The output labels of both methods are combined by multiplication. In summary, the label propagation spatially localises and divides the hyperintensity regions detected by kmeans. All steps were implemented based on MIRTK toolbox [3]. We run the label generation pipeline for 80 term and 40 preterm datasets. The output labels were then visually inspected and manually refined in ITK-SNAP, when required.

Preprocessing and Training of UNETR Segmentation Model: The preprocessing of the datasets (T2w images and PWM labels) for training included masking using the DRAW-EM brain mask, cropping of the background and resampling with padding to $160 \times 160 \times 160$ grid. We used 90 datasets for training and 10 for validation (including term and preterm). The training was performed for 20000 iterations with the standard MONAI augmentation (random bias field, contrast adjustment, Gaussian noise and affine rotations $\pm 45°$).

Evaluation of UNETR Segmentation: The performance was tested on 10 term and 10 preterm datasets qualitatively in terms of the PWM region detection status (visual assessment: correct = 100%, partial = 50%, failed = 0%), and quantitatively by comparison to the ground truth labels in terms of recall, precision and Dice as well as the relative difference in volume and T2 signal intensity.

2.4   Quantitative Analysis of PWM in Term and Preterm Cohorts

The feasibility of using the proposed segmentation pipeline for quantitative studies was assessed based on comparison of term and preterm MRI datasets. We used the trained network to segment 150 term and 50 preterm subjects. The PWM segmentations were used to compute ROI-specific values including volumetry and mean DTI indices (fractional anisotropy (FA) and mean diffusivity (MD)). The scripts for all calculations were implemented in MIRTK toolbox [3].

3   Results and Discussion

3.1   Parcellation Map of Periventricular WM ROIs in the Atlas Space

Figure 4 shows the first formalised 3D parcellation map for five periventricular WM regions (with left/right separation) along with the original T2w atlas [26]. The segmented regions follow the definitions from [15,23] that call these regions "periventricular crossroads": C1, C2, C4, C5 and C6. The C2 and C5 ROIs have the expected "horn" shape. All PWM ROIs have the pronounced brighter T2 intensity, which is expected to correspond to the higher water content of PWM tissue [15,26]. The segmentations were inspected and confirmed by two clinicians with extensive experience in neonatal brain MRI.

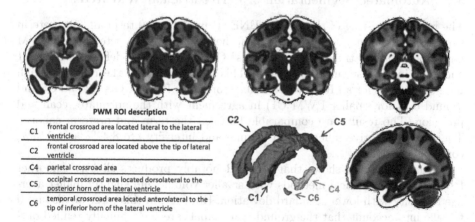

PWM ROI description

C1	frontal crossroad area located lateral to the lateral ventricle
C2	frontal crossroad area located above the tip of lateral ventricle
C4	parietal crossroad area
C5	occipital crossroad area located dorsolateral to the posterior horn of the lateral ventricle
C6	temporal crossroad area located anterolateral to the tip of inferior horn of the lateral ventricle

Fig. 4. The parcellation map of five periventricular WM regions created in the T2w neonatal brain atlas space [26]. Based on the original definitions in [15,23], these ROIs are referred to as periventricular "crossroads": C1, C2, C4, C5 and C6.

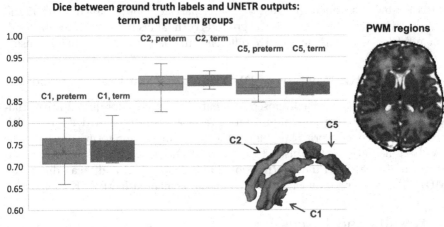

Fig. 5. Quantitative assessment of the trained UNETR model for segmentation of three PWM regions based on the comparison with the ground truth labels on 10 term and 10 preterm test subjects. The metrics (Dice, recall, precision, relative volume and intensity difference) were calculated for combined left and right PWM ROI labels.

3.2   Automated Segmentation of Periventricular WM ROIs

The results of testing of the trained UNETR model on 10 term and 10 preterm subjects are summarised in Fig. 5. The network correctly detected all PWM regions selected for training ("crossroads" C1, C2 and C5 as defined in Sect. 3.1 and [23]) in all test subjects (100%). This is confirmed by the relatively high Dice coefficients for all ROIs (around 0.88 for larger PWM ROIs C2 and C5 and around 0.74 for smaller PWM C1) in agreement with the adequate recall and precision. The results are comparable between the term and preterm cohorts. The average relative difference in volume and intensity are 8.42% and 0.87%, correspondingly.

Visual inspection shows that UNETR notably produces slightly smoother labels than the classical methods with smaller volume and slightly higher average intensity with lower standard deviation. However, in this case, we also need to take into account that the ground truth labels are the manually refined outputs of the combined kmeans and label propagation segmentation. Notably, only minimal manual correction was required in 25.4% of all cases primarily when the input WM DRAW-EM labels were incorrect in the ventricle regions and for the late PMA and preterm cases with less pronounced PWM ROIs boundaries. At the same time, neither manual or automated segmentations cannot be

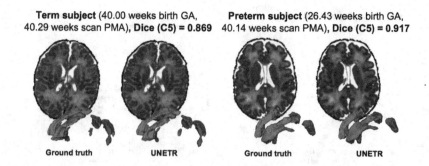

Fig. 6. An example of the difference between the ground truth and UNETR output labels for test term and preterm subjects.

considered as the absolute ground truth because there is no precise definition of the correct PWM delineation due to the blurred boundaries, patchy appearance and the transient nature of this WM compartment. This is potentially the main cause of the difference between the ground truth and UNETR label volumes. This is illustrated in Fig. 6 that shows an example of the difference between the ground truth and UNETR output labels for one of the subjects.

3.3   Quantitative Analysis of PWM in Term and Preterm Cohorts

Figure 7 shows the results of comparison between 150 term and 50 preterm subjects based on volumetry and diffusion MRI metrics derived from the UNETR PWM segmentations (the analysis was performed for C2 frontal ROI only). All automated segmentations were reviewed and confirmed as acceptable. Additional minor manual refinements were required in 17.5% of cases, which notably did not affect the trends in any of the metrics.

The term cohort is characterised by the pronounced decrease in both absolute and relative PWM volume (that correlates with the increasing total WM volume) along with the decreasing MD and increasing FA, which are the expected changes in maturing WM. On the other hand, there are no prominent (significant) trends for the preterm subjects in any of the metrics. The difference between the term and preterm cohort trends is significant ($p < 0.001$) only in the intensity metrics. The group of preterm subjects have the higher MD and T2 values and lower FA than in the term cohort. This is potentially related to the higher water content due to the prolonged existence of transient WM in the preterm brain [11, 16,23]. This also is in agreement with the results reported in [26]. However, taking into account the smaller number of available preterm subjects (50), the heterogeneity of the cohort and the respective variations in the GA at birth (24–32 weeks GA, Fig. 2), a more comprehensive investigation on a larger cohort is required for further analysis of correlations between the age at birth and PWM characteristics.

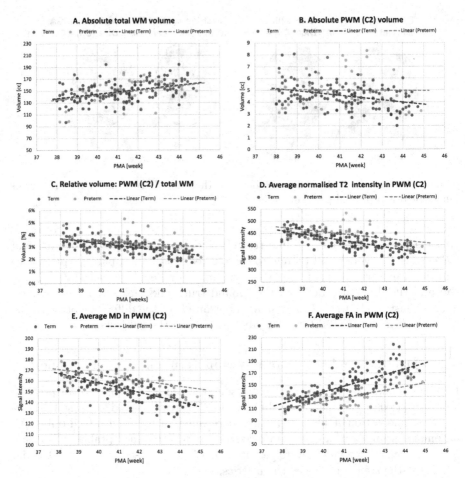

Fig. 7. Comparison between term (150, blue) and preterm (50, red) cohorts (dHCP datasets): volumetry and dMRI metrics computed for UNETR PWM segmentations (C2 ROI). (Color figure online)

4   Conclusions

In summary, we presented the first deep learning solution for automated multi-label segmentation of periventricular WM regions in neonatal T2w brain MRI. This included formalisation and definition of the PWM parcellation map in the standard atlas space. In addition, we demonstrated the feasibility of using semi-automated combination of kmeans and label propagation for generation of PWM labels for training the of the networks, which significantly decreases the preparation time in comparison to manual labels. The practicability of using deep learning (UNETR) for PWM segmentation was confirmed by quantitative comparison of 200 term and preterm subjects from dHCP cohort. The results of the analysis showed a significant difference in volumetry and mean DTI indices withing PWM regions. There are also pronounced trends in PWM-derived metrics vs. PMA for the term cohort. Our future work will focus on further automation of parcellation of the rest of the WM tissue types (e.g., subplate), optimisation for different acquisition protocols and wider PMA range and a large scale quantitative analysis.

Acknowledgments. We thank everyone who was involved in acquisition and analysis of the datasets as a part of dHCP project. We thank all participants and their families.

This work was supported by the Academy of Medical Sciences Springboard Award (SBF004\1040), the European Research Council under the European Union's Seventh Framework Programme [FP7/ 20072013]/ERC grant agreement no. 319456 dHCP project, the Wellcome/EPSRC Centre for Medical Engineering at King's College London [WT 203148/Z/16/Z)], the NIHR Clinical Research Facility (CRF) at Guy's and St Thomas' and by the National Institute for Health Research Biomedical Research Centre based at Guy's and St Thomas' NHS Foundation Trust and King's College London.

The views expressed are those of the authors and not necessarily those of the NHS, the NIHR or the Department of Health.

References

1. Developing human connectome project. http://www.developingconnectome.org
2. ITK-snap segmentation tool. http://www.itksnap.org
3. MIRTK Software Package. https://github.com/BioMedIA/MIRTK
4. MONAI Framework. https://github.com/Project-MONAI/MONAI
5. Alexander, B., et al.: White matter extension of the Melbourne children's regional infant brain atlas: M-CRIB-WM. Hum. Brain Mapp. **41**, 2317–2333 (2020)
6. Beare, R.J., et al.: Neonatal brain tissue classification with morphological adaptation and unified segmentation. Front. Neuroinform. **10** (2016)
7. Christiaens, D., et al.: Scattered slice SHARD reconstruction for motion correction in multi-shell diffusion MRI. NeuroImage **225**, 117437 (2021)
8. Cordero-Grande, L., et al.: Three-dimensional motion corrected sensitivity encoding reconstruction for multi-shot multi-slice MRI: application to neonatal brain imaging. Magn. Reson. Med. **79**(3), 1365–1376 (2018)
9. Dubois, J., et al.: MRI of the neonatal brain: a review of methodological challenges and neuroscientific advances. J. Magn. Reson. Imaging **53**, 1318–1343 (2021)
10. Fan, X., et al.: Attention-modulated multi-branch convolutional neural networks for neonatal brain tissue segmentation. Comput. Biol. Med. **146** (2022)
11. Girard, N., et al.: MRI assessment of neonatal brain maturation. Imaging Med. **4**(6), 613–632 (2012)
12. Grigorescu, I., et al.: Harmonized segmentation of neonatal brain MRI. Front. Neurosci. **15**, 565 (2021)
13. Hatamizadeh, A., et al.: UNETR: transformers for 3D medical image segmentation. In: 2022 IEEE/CVF WACV, pp. 1748–1758 (2022)
14. Hughes, E.J., et al.: A dedicated neonatal brain imaging system. Magn. Reson. Med. **78**(2), 794–804 (2017)
15. Judaš, M., et al.: Structural, immunocytochemical, and MR imaging properties of periventricular crossroads of growing cortical pathways in preterm infants. Am. J. Neuroradiol. **26**, 2671–2684 (2005)

16. Kostović, I., Judaš, M.: Prolonged coexistence of transient and permanent circuitry elements in the developing cerebral cortex of fetuses and preterm infants. Dev. Med. Child Neurol. **48**, 388–393 (2006)
17. Kostović, I., et al.: Developmental dynamics of radial vulnerability in the cerebral compartments in preterm infants and neonates. Front. Neuroi. **5**, 1–13 (2014)
18. Kuklisova-Murgasova, M., et al.: A dynamic 4d probabilistic atlas of the developing brain. Neuroimage **54**, 2750–2763 (2011)
19. Kuklisova-Murgasova, M., et al.: Reconstruction of fetal brain MRI with intensity matching and complete outlier removal. Media **16**(8), 1550–1564 (2012)
20. Li, H., et al.: Objective and automated detection of diffuse white matter abnormality in preterm infants using deep convolutional neural networks. Front. Neurosci. **13**, 1–12 (2019)
21. Makropoulos, A., et al.: Automatic whole brain mri segmentation of the developing neonatal brain. IEEE TMI **33**, 1818–1831 (2014)
22. Parikh, N.A., et al.: Automatically quantified DEHSI on MRI predicts cognitive development in preterm infants. Pediatr. Neurol. **49**, 424–430 (2013)
23. Pittet, M.P., et al.: Newborns and preterm infants at term equivalent age: A semi-quantitative assessment of cerebral maturity. Neuroimage **24**, 102014 (2019)
24. Schuh, A., et al.: Unbiased construction of a temporally consistent morphological atlas of neonatal brain development. bioRxiv pp. 2–66 (2018)
25. Tournier, J.D., et al.: Mrtrix3: a fast, flexible and open software framework for medical image processing and visualisation. Neuroimage **202** (2019)
26. Uus, A., et al.: Multi-channel 4d parametrized atlas of macro- and microstructural neonatal brain development. Front. Neurosci. **15**, 721 (2021)

Knowledge-Guided Segmentation
of Isointense Infant Brain

Jana Vujadinovic[1,2]($\boxtimes$), Jaime Simarro Viana[1,3], Ezequiel de la Rosa[1,4],
Els Ortibus[3,5], and Diana M. Sima[1]

[1] icometrix, Leuven, Belgium
janavujadinovic@outlook.com
[2] Erasmus Joint Master in Medical Imaging and Applications, University of Girona,
Girona, Spain
[3] Department of Development and Regeneration, KU Leuven, Leuven, Belgium
[4] Department of Computer Science, Technical University of Munich,
Munich, Germany
[5] Department of Pediatric Neurology, UZ Leuven, Leuven, Belgium

Abstract. Tissue segmentation of infants could lead to early diagnosis
of neurological disorders, potentially enabling early interventions. However, the challenge of tissue quantification is increased due to the very
dynamic changes that happen as brain development advances over the
course of the first year. One of the structural processes is the myelination
which causes limited contrast between gray and white matter tissue on
T1-weighted and T2-weighted magnetic resonance images at around six
to nine months. In recent years, as a result of the MICCAI brain MRI
segmentation challenge in 6-month old infants (iSeg17 and iSeg19), there
has been an increase in interest in this complex task. In this work, we propose two methodologies to overcome issues of erroneous segmentation on
the border between gray and white matter, based on knowledge-guided
U-Net for segmenting the isointense infant brain. First, segmentation was
guided using a prior of white matter obtained from an atlas for developing
infants. Second, segmentation was focused on the low-intensity contrast
boundary between white and gray matter. Experimental results on the
subjects of iSeg19 challenge display the potential of utilizing the white
matter prior as input for segmentation. Overall, its utilization leads to
results that are closer to the brain anatomy with smoother and connected
white matter regions.

Keywords: Guided segmentation · Isointense phase · Brain
quantification

1 Introduction

Magnetic resonance imaging (MRI) allows the study of the brain in-vivo. Neurological disorders could potentially be identified before their onset by detecting

The original version of this chapter was revised: this paper was unfortunately published
without Acknowledgement. This has been updated. The correction to this chapter is
available at https://doi.org/10.1007/978-3-031-17117-8_11

R. Licandro et al. (Eds.): PIPPI 2022, LNCS 13575, pp. 105–114, 2022.
https://doi.org/10.1007/978-3-031-17117-8_10

brain anomalies [8]. Specifically, MRI quantification of the brain tissues (i.e., white matter (WM) and gray matter (GM)) has been proven to be helpful for the early detection of neurological disorders such as schizophrenia [6] and autism [7].

Despite the potential clinical value of developing automatic methods in infants, MRI quantification of very young patients (i.e., from birth to 2 years old) presents multiple challenges. Infant MR scans suffer from lower quality as a result of increased partial volume effect due to smaller brain size, and motion artifacts [25]. In addition, rapid and non-linear neurodevelopmental changes contribute to heterogeneous intensities in MR images leading to unclear borders between GM and WM and regional variations in contrast [16]. Furthermore, equipment manufacturers, magnetic field strength, and acquisition protocol can affect the contrast and intensity distribution in acquired images leading to multi-site heterogeneity issues [19].

The isointense phase occurs at around 6 to 9 months of age and is defined as the period when GM and WM intensities overlap (see Fig. 1). The myelination, which progresses from central to peripheral brain regions, causes GM and WM to exhibit similar intensities (in both T1-weighted and T2-weighted images). As a result of limited contrast between GM and WM, tissue quantification is extremely challenging.

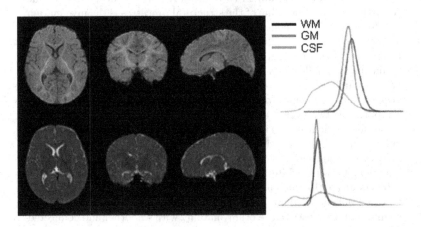

Fig. 1. Brain MRI in the isointense phase of brain development. The first row displays T1-weighted images and the second-row T2-weighted images in axial, coronal, sagittal view and corresponding tissue intensity distributions, respectively.

Previous research in the isointense brain segmentation can be split into three categories: atlas-based methods, learning-based methods, and hybrid approaches. Employing atlas-based methods depends highly on the present contrast in the MR images and can be time-consuming [25]. Learning based-methods are further split into machine learning [21,22] and deep learning methods [2,5,10], with some deep learning methods employing the longitudinal data to guide the segmentation [3]. Generally, deep learning methods enable automatic learning of more representative and discriminative features, whereas classical machine learning methods require explicit data characterization through hand-crafted features [4,11,13]. Alternatively, hybrid approaches [18] integrate multiple strategies into a final pipeline.

Deep learning-based networks have a consistently good performance. However, they suffer from persistent errors present at the border between GM and WM. Recent works demonstrate the potential of utilizing prior anatomical knowledge to guide the segmentation. For example, Kushibar et al. [9] utilize spatial features extracted from a structural probabilistic atlas to guide the segmentation in sub-cortical brain structure. Furthermore, Wang et al. [22,23] introduce a signed distance map in a two-stage sequential segmentation process. The signed distance maps assure the presence of WM inside GM and guide the final segmentation result.

Inspired by these approaches and considering there are numerous ways of introducing prior information, two new methodologies are proposed for dealing with the isointense stage of brain development. The first adds prior information regarding WM localization obtained from an atlas, in combination with T1-weighted and T2-weighted images as input to a neural network. This approach uses previously defined tissue labels on reference MR images (i.e. atlas) as prior knowledge to segment a target image. In the second method, inspired by the works of Navarro et al. in multi-organ segmentation [14], we define modeling the boundary between gray and white matter to guide the segmentation in unclear regions.

2 Methodology

2.1 Dataset and Atlas

iSeg19 is a publicly available dataset provided by MICCAI challenge [19]. This dataset consists of T1-weighted and T2-weighted images of infants aged 6 ± 0.8 months. The fully pre-processed dataset (resampled, skull-stripped, with corrected inhomogeneities and cerebelllum and brain stem removed) consists of ten training samples containing both intensity and ground truth (GT) images and thirteen cases of only intensity images for validation. Experiments were performed on the training dataset and the best-performing pipeline was further tested on the validation dataset.

Annotation of CSF, WM, and GM of the dataset was done by the iSeg19 challenge organizers.

Atlas for developing infants provided by Zhang et al. (2016) [24] gives information on common brain anatomy of 6 months old infants in standardized space.

2.2 Data Preparation

Pre-processing the data reduces the variability across subjects. Firstly, in each image, the intensities above the 99 percentile and below 1 percentile were cropped, removing the influence of outliers. Secondly, a min-max normalization was used to scale the values between 0 and 1. Finally, a data augmentation technique of flipping was implemented to increase the number of volumes during training. The dataset was doubled by including left-to-right flipped volumes in training, taking into account the pseudo-symmetrical nature of the left and right hemispheres of the brain.

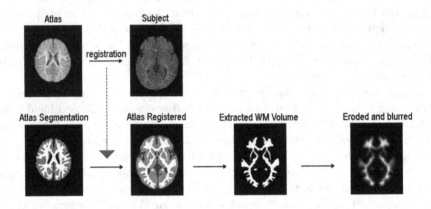

Fig. 2. Pipeline for extracting prior information from the atlas

Anatomical Prior was derived utilizing image registration to align the atlas and the particular subject. Specifically, the T1-weighted image of the subject and the T1-weighted atlas were registered. A sequential process of implementing affine [15] and non-rigid [12] registrations was used to provide the deformation map for label propagation of the atlas segmentation to the subject space. The propagation of the labels was followed by extracting only the WM segmentation and processing it using erosion and Gaussian blurring. The initial usage of erosion was done given the imperfect alignment between the ground truth and the propagated labels. The Gaussian blurring was implemented to smooth the anatomical prior. The blurring level was manually adjusted trying to preserve reasonable information, sigma was set to 3.

Patch Extraction technique was employed as a result of limited number of samples available for training. The overlap was introduced by decreasing the patch stride to be smaller than the patch size, with the patch size being $16 \times 16 \times 16$ and patch stride $8 \times 8 \times 8$. Only patches that include at least a predefined portion of genuine brain volume were considered in training.

2.3   Deep Learning Network

U-Net is a well-known state-of-the-art deep learning network for biomedical image segmentation [17]. This network has been extensively used to segment the isointense phase of brain development [19,23].

Training parameters utilized for both networks explained in the next two subsections include Adam optimizer, batch size of 32 and 100 epochs with early stopping. Furthermore, dropout is introduced to prevent overfitting.

The following two networks were developed and tested:

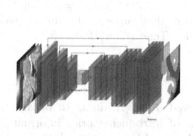 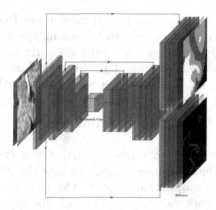

(a) U-Net model used for segmentation with WM prior as third input channel.

(b) Multi-branch U-Net model with two outputs, segmentation and contour prediction.

Fig. 3. Illustrations of U-Net architectures developed

I. White Matter Prior. In this case the U-Net network (Fig. 3a) is trained using three inputs, T1-weighted, T2-weighted and WM prior information acquired from an atlas. The loss function is categorical cross-entropy.

II. Multi-branch U-Net. We develop a complementary learning task where second to last decoder block splits into two separate decoder blocks each with its own softmax activation function. The segmentation is output by one, while the contour representing the boundary between gray and white matter is output by the other. As there are two separate outputs, the optimized loss function is the sum of objectives of the related tasks, i.e., segmentation (categorical cross-entropy) and contour prediction (binary cross-entropy).

$$L_{total} = L_{tissue} + L_{contour}$$

$$L_{tissue} = -\sum_{c=1}^{M}\sum_{o=1}^{N} y_{o,c} \log(p_{o,c})$$

$$L_{contour} = -\sum_{c=1}^{M} (y_c \log(p) + (1 - y_c) \log(1 - p))$$

where M - number of classes, N - number of observations, y - binary indicator (0 or 1) if class label c is the correct classification for observation o, and p - predicted probability that observation o is of class c.

2.4   Implementation Details

This project was implemented using Python programming language. Complementary libraries used include numpy, nibabel, patchify and matplotlib. Image registration was done using icometrix's implementation of NiftyReg [12,15]. Erosion and blurring of the registered atlas were done using scikit-image package [20]. The 3D U-Net was implemented using Tensorflow [1].

3   Experiments and Results

A leave-one-out cross-validation was employed during training to obtain the optimal parameters and evaluate the effects of introducing prior information. Nine subjects would be used for training and one subject for testing. During the network training, the training subjects would be further split using an 80%/20% strategy. The metric used for evaluation of training results is Dice similarity coefficient (DSC). For the validation dataset of the challenge, as provided by the challenge's organizers once the segmentation results have been submitted, the metrics also include 95th percentile Hausdorff distance (HD) and average surface distance (ASD).

Once labels of the atlas have been propagated to the patient space using distinct deformation maps, five experiments were performed as follows: i) baseline U-Net (using no prior information); ii) using WM prior; iii) using GM prior on WM prior trained network to observe if the network is utilizing the WM information for prediction; iv) using *perfect* prior which is obtained from the ground truth to observe the potential result in case of *perfect* image registration and v) adding contour to guide the segmentation.

Quantitative Results. Figure 4 illustrates effects of adding prior information. Employing the WM prior as an extra input channel leads to a slight increase in the WM and GM DSC value when compared to the baseline U-Net. The utilization of the prior by the network is further confirmed when using the GM prior for prediction on a WM prior trained network. In this case, we attribute the small decrease in DSC for CSF to the prior not affecting that location, and a considerable decrease of 16.1% for GM and 25.1% for WM to the effect of using misleading information as input. The potential of utilizing this type of information is further tested when utilizing the *perfect* prior obtained from the GT and processed in the same manner as previously explained. In this case, an increase of 0.9% in the case of CSF, 4.5% in the case of GM, and 7.2% in the case of WM when compared to the results of the model "With Prior" information is observed. In contrast, complementary task learning (i.e., adding the WM/GM contour as second output) did not improve the results.

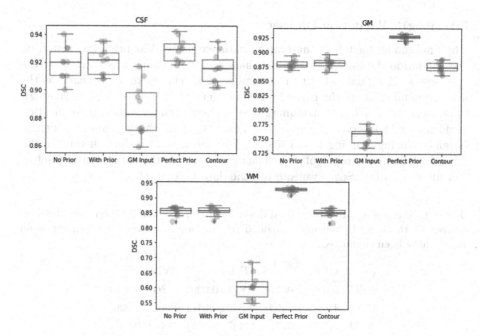

Fig. 4. Value of DSC for different tissue classes for each one of the experiments on the training dataset showcased on x-axis.

Qualitative Results. Figure 5 shows a qualitative comparison between using the baseline network and the networks guided by the prior. The WM prior obtained with label propagation leads to more anatomically accurate results similar to those present in GT with smooth and connected WM regions as we can observe from the highlighted regions.

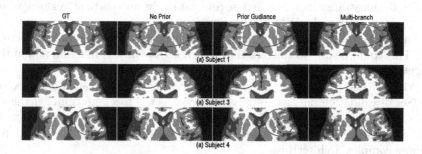

Fig. 5. Qualitative improvement in segmentation when using the WM prior. The 1st column shows the GT, 2nd column showcases the segmentation results of the baseline U-Net with no prior information, 3rd column when using the WM prior obtained with the label propagation, and 4th column displays the multi-branch U-Net.

3.1   iSeg19 Validation Dataset

The final model including anatomical guidance using WM prior was tested on the validation dataset of the iSeg19 challenge. This model was trained on the complete training dataset with the number of epochs set to 42 as that was the average number of epochs needed for convergence in the leave-one-out strategy.

As a result of adequate training (avoiding over-fitting), a good generalization performance is observed, since the segmentation results are coherent with those obtained during training (see Table 1). Furthermore, Hausdorff distance (HD) for WM falls in the top 4 of the challenge results on the validation dataset as consulted from the iSeg19 website (on the date 11/07/2022).

Table 1. Average mean and standard deviation DSC, HD, and ASD on the validation dataset of the iSeg19 challenge, provided by the organizers once the segmentation results have been submitted.

	CSF	GM	WM
DSC	0.927 (0.007)	0.891 (0.009)	0.860 (0.016)
HD	10.023 (1.659)	7.340 (1.247)	6.659 (1.020)
ASD	0.197 (0.017)	0.437 (0.038)	0.499 (0.048)

4   Discussion and Conclusions

In this work, we propose a solution for introducing prior information to the challenging task of segmenting infant tissue in the isointense phase, characterized by the limited distinction between GM and WM tissue on T1-weighted and T2-weighted images.

Overall, experimental results on the iSeg19 dataset showcase a slight increase in performance when utilizing the WM tissue prior. Visual analysis of the above results demonstrates more refined segmentation in sub-cortical regions when using information of the WM localization.

The multi-branch U-Net did not perform better than the proposed alternative. This could be due to the fact that the choice of the loss function and of the weighting between the two losses was not fully optimized.

With the exception of the Hausdorff distance metric, the results obtained on the iSeg19 validation dataset were not good as the top performing challenge participants. This might be explained by the fact that we used an easy-too-train and well-established U-net network that is presumably less optimized compared to more complex architectures.

The presented work is limited to the data only related to the 6-month old infants, although the isointense phase occurs at around 6 to 9 months. Furthermore, the developed method requires both T1 and T2-weighted images. Future work includes further improving the registration between the atlas and the specific subject as well as optimizing the network, considering a simple U-Net architecture was implemented to test the effect of this type of prior.

Acknowledgement. The PARENT project has received funding from the European Union's Horizon 2020 research and innovation program under the Marie Sklodowska-Curie Innovative Training Network 2020. Grant Agreement N 956394.

References

1. Abadi, M., et al.: TensorFlow: large-scale machine learning on heterogeneous systems (2015). https://www.tensorflow.org/, software available from tensorflow.org
2. Bui, T.D., Shin, J., Moon, T.: 3D densely convolutional networks for volumetric segmentation. arXiv preprint arXiv:1709.03199 (2017)
3. Bui, T.D., Wang, L., Lin, W., Li, G., Shen, D.: 6-month infant brain MRI segmentation guided by 24-month data using cycle-consistent adversarial networks. In: 2020 IEEE 17th International Symposium on Biomedical Imaging (ISBI), pp. 359–362. IEEE (2020)
4. Castiglioni, I., et al.: AI applications to medical images: from machine learning to deep learning. Physica Med. **83**, 9–24 (2021)
5. Dolz, J., et al.: Deep CNN ensembles and suggestive annotations for infant brain MRI segmentation. Comput. Med. Imaging Graph. **79** (2020)
6. Gilmore, J.H., et al.: Prenatal and neonatal brain structure and white matter maturation in children at high risk for schizophrenia. Am. J. Psychiatry **167**(9), 1083–1091 (2010)
7. Hazlett, H.C., et al.: Magnetic resonance imaging and head circumference study of brain size in autism: birth through age 2 years. Arch. Gen. Psychiatry **62**(12), 1366–1376 (2005)
8. Knickmeyer, R.C., et al.: A structural MRI study of human brain development from birth to 2 years. J. Neurosci. **28**(47), 12176–12182 (2008)
9. Kushibar, K., et al.: Automated sub-cortical brain structure segmentation combining spatial and deep convolutional features. Med. Image Anal. **48**, 177–186 (2018)
10. Lei, Z., Qi, L., Wei, Y., Zhou, Y.: Infant brain MRI segmentation with dilated convolution pyramid downsampling and self-attention. arXiv preprint arXiv:1912.12570 (2019)
11. Li, G., et al.: Computational neuroanatomy of baby brains: a review. Neuroimage **185**, 906–925 (2019)
12. Modat, M., Ridgway, G.R., Taylor, Z.A., Lehmann, M., Barnes, J., Hawkes, D.J., Fox, N.C., Ourselin, S.: Fast free-form deformation using graphics processing units. Comput. Methods Programs Biomed. **98**(3), 278–284 (2010)
13. Moeskops, P., Viergever, M.A., Mendrik, A.M., De Vries, L.S., Benders, M.J., Išgum, I.: Automatic segmentation of MR brain images with a convolutional neural network. IEEE Trans. Med. Imaging **35**(5), 1252–1261 (2016)
14. Navarro, F., et al.: Shape-aware complementary-task learning for multi-organ segmentation. In: Suk, H.-I., Liu, M., Yan, P., Lian, C. (eds.) MLMI 2019. LNCS, vol. 11861, pp. 620–627. Springer, Cham (2019). https://doi.org/10.1007/978-3-030-32692-0_71
15. Ourselin, S., Roche, A., Subsol, G., Pennec, X., Ayache, N.: Reconstructing a 3D structure from serial histological sections. Image Vis. Comput. **19**(1–2), 25–31 (2001)
16. Paus, T., Collins, D., Evans, A., Leonard, G., Pike, B., Zijdenbos, A.: Maturation of white matter in the human brain: a review of magnetic resonance studies. Brain Res. Bull. **54**(3), 255–266 (2001)

17. Ronneberger, O., Fischer, P., Brox, T.: U-Net: convolutional networks for biomedical image segmentation. In: Navab, N., Hornegger, J., Wells, W.M., Frangi, A.F. (eds.) MICCAI 2015. LNCS, vol. 9351, pp. 234–241. Springer, Cham (2015). https://doi.org/10.1007/978-3-319-24574-4_28

18. Sanroma, G., Benkarim, O.M., Piella, G., Ballester, M.Á.G.: Building an ensemble of complementary segmentation methods by exploiting probabilistic estimates. In: Wang, L., Adeli, E., Wang, Q., Shi, Y., Suk, H.-I. (eds.) MLMI 2016. LNCS, vol. 10019, pp. 27–35. Springer, Cham (2016). https://doi.org/10.1007/978-3-319-47157-0_4

19. Sun, Y., et al.: Multi-site infant brain segmentation algorithms: the iSeg-2019 challenge. IEEE Trans. Med. Imaging 40(5), 1363–1376 (2021)

20. van der Walt, S., et al.: The scikit-image contributors: scikit-image: image processing in Python. Peer J. 2, (2014). https://doi.org/10.7717/peerj.453

21. Wang, I., et al.: Links: learning-based multi-source IntegratioN framework for segmentation of infant brain images. Neuroimage 108, 160–172 (2015)

22. Wang, I., et al.: Anatomy-guided joint tissue segmentation and topological correction for 6-month infant brain MRI with risk of autism. Hum. Brain Mapp. 39(6), 2609–2623 (2018)

23. Wang, L., et al.: Volume-based analysis of 6-month-old infant brain MRI for autism biomarker identification and early diagnosis. In: Frangi, A.F., Schnabel, J.A., Davatzikos, C., Alberola-López, C., Fichtinger, G. (eds.) MICCAI 2018. LNCS, vol. 11072, pp. 411–419. Springer, Cham (2018). https://doi.org/10.1007/978-3-030-00931-1_47

24. Zhang, Y., Shi, F., Wu, G., Wang, L., Yap, P.T., Shen, D.: Consistent spatial-temporal longitudinal atlas construction for developing infant brains. IEEE Trans. Med. Imaging 35(12), 2568–2577 (2016)

25. Zöllei, L., Iglesias, J.E., Ou, Y., Grant, P.E., Fischl, B.: Infant FreeSurfer: an automated segmentation and surface extraction pipeline for T1-weighted neuroimaging data of infants 0–2 years. Neuroimage 218 (2020)

Correction to: Knowledge-Guided Segmentation of Isointense Infant Brain

Jana Vujadinovic, Jaime Simarro Viana, Ezequiel de la Rosa,
Els Ortibus, and Diana M. Sima

Correction to:
Chapter "Knowledge-Guided Segmentation of Isointense
Infant Brain" in: R. Licandro et al. (Eds.): *Perinatal,*
***Preterm and Paediatric Image Analysis*, LNCS 13575,**
https://doi.org/10.1007/978-3-031-17117-8_10

.

The original version of this paper was unfortunately published without Acknowledgement. This has been updated.

The updated original version of this chapter can be found at
https://doi.org/10.1007/978-3-031-17117-8_10

Author Index

Printed in the United States
by Baker & Taylor Publisher Services